The Captain's Daughters

DOREEN D. BERGER

Copyright © 2021 by Doreen D. Berger

All rights reserved. No part of this publication may be reproduced, distributed, or transmitted in any form or by any means, including photocopying, recording, or other electronic or mechanical methods, without the prior written permission of the publisher, except in the case of brief quotations embodied in critical reviews and certain other noncommercial uses permitted by copyright law.

To request permissions, contact the publisher at *info@PolarisPrintBooks.com.*

The characters and events portrayed in this book are fictitious or are used fictitiously. Any similarity to real persons, living or dead, is purely coincidental and not intended by the author.

Paperback: 978-1-7365421-0-1
Ebook: 978-1-7365421-1-8

Library of Congress Control Number: 2021902932

First paperback edition April 2021.

Edited by Elisa Drake
Cover art by Damonza.com
Layout by Damonza.com

Published by PolarisPrint, LLC
East Meadow, New York

PolarisPrintBooks.com

TABLE OF CONTENTS

Polaris is a very special star........................vii
Chapter 1: A Morning Ride 1
Chapter 2: Trouble on the Polaris...................14
Chapter 3: The Search 22
Chapter 4: The Alien Ship 31
Chapter 5: Despicable 40
Chapter 6: Peanut Butter and Pizza 44
Chapter 7: Can You Finger Dance? 50
Chapter 8: Milk…No Way! 60
Chapter 9: Looking Back...........................66
Chapter 10: Starbase Sesta VI......................84
Chapter 11: The Babysitting Caper 89
Chapter 12: Unspoken Possibilities 107
Chapter 13: A Very Tall Tale......................111
Chapter 14: The Twilight Zone 123
Chapter 15: Never Even in the Realm of Possibility 136
Chapter 16: But He Looks Like Dad 151
Chapter 17: What If...............................173
Chapter 18: A New Polaris.........................181
Chapter 19: Let Your Guard Down 188

Chapter 20: Zuralite Crystals............................192
Chapter 21: A Saras Fairy..........................208
Chapter 22: A Tiny Spider.........................218
Chapter 23: Pizza Pies...Again.....................227
Chapter 24: Dad Waits............................230
Chapter 25: Fatherhood...........................234
Chapter 26: Dad, I Know What I Want to Be 238
Chapter 27: The Dreaded Injector 243
Chapter 28: Captured 250
Chapter 29: Jastar................................258
Chapter 30: Unstoppable Together..................275
Chapter 31: The Brig.............................290
Chapter 32: Crossing Over........................298
Chapter 33: Dad Heads to the Portal 308
Chapter 34: Attack...............................312
Chapter 35: The Charade.........................315
Chapter 36: Homecoming 321
About the Author................................332

For my father…my daddy…my hero.

and

For Robin…These 75,064 words could not begin to express what your friendship means to me.

Polaris is a very special star.

Polaris can be found almost directly above the North Pole and is, therefore, nicknamed the North Star or Pole Star. It can be easily located as it is the brightest star in the constellation Ursa Minor (the Little Bear), and is the last star in the handle of the Little Dipper. As the Earth turns, Polaris appears to remain stationary and all the stars appear to rotate around it. It is the only star in the sky to have this unique characteristic, and since its stationary position points due north, Polaris can be used for navigation in the Northern Hemisphere.

For centuries, explorers need only look to the heavens, and to Polaris, to find their way safely home.

CHAPTER 1

A Morning Ride

March, 2297, Santa Fe, New Mexico

"Dad, we know what to do!" Diane assured him again, totally exasperated, as he gave her and Robin last-minute instructions. "We're twelve!" she reminded him. "We don't need your help! Honestly, we don't."

Captain William Marsh responded to his daughter's remark with a fatherly grin. "Oh, really? I'll keep that in mind the next time you request my assistance." Then he rechecked the horses' saddles and helped the girls mount anyway.

Diane looked at her younger sister and shook her head in amused disbelief. Robin smiled back and nodded in understanding…they had been raised on a horse ranch and could do all of this independently.

"Why don't you come with us, Dad?" Robin asked for the second time when he'd finished fussing with her stirrups.

He looked up at them, smiled, and almost said yes, but then firmly shook his head no. "Thanks for the invitation. I wish I could, but I have work to do. You two go on by yourselves. We'll take a ride together tomorrow. Maybe we'll pack a picnic lunch and stay out all afternoon."

Forgetting her earlier frustration, Diane nodded enthusiastically and gave him a bright smile. "Really? That would be great!" She reached over to scratch her horse's neck and whispered into his black-tipped ear, "We'd like that, wouldn't we, Pepper?" The gray Quarter Horse replied by stamping his hoof in the sand and flinging his majestic head. "Yep, he wants to go, Dad," she translated playfully.

"We're going to hold you to it, Daddy," Robin told him adamantly. "We're supposed to be on shore leave, but you've been working all week." She tried to keep from laughing as she leaned down from her vantage point astride her white horse, shook her finger at him, and said as seriously as she could, "You'd *better* finish up today."

"Yes, Ma'am," he answered, chuckling and saluting up to her. "Go," he said to his daughters. "Have a nice morning and be back in time for lunch. Do you have your communication badges?"

"Yes, Dad," Diane said, getting impatient again.

"Good. Contact me if you need to."

"We will, Dad. We know the drill," Diane answered sharply, rolling her eyes at him even though she knew it irked him when she did.

Ignoring her sass, he looked up at her and continued, "Go only to the creek and nowhere else."

Robin jumped in before her sister said something that might get her grounded. "Okay, Dad, we got it."

He nodded, satisfied that his instructions were understood and then added, "And behave yourselves! Stay out of trouble. I'm not kidding."

"We will," Robin promised as she and her sister both nodded and smiled angelically at him...too angelically for his comfort. He'd heard *that* promise before—more times than he cared to count.

Diane and Robin had such a knack for finding mischief.

"Bye, Daddy. See you later," the girls chorused as they rode off. When they reached the ranch gate, they turned and waved to him. He saw they were already deep in conversation and giggling about something or other.

Both had bright eyes and a head of curls—Diane's dark, Robin's a rich honey color—but it was their laughter he loved the most. They would giggle at just about anything, with laughter so contagious he ended up laughing with them. He found it hard to be stern if they started to laugh because if he didn't concentrate, he'd get sucked right into their fun and forget whatever lesson he was trying to teach. It was the sound he missed the most when he wasn't with them.

He smiled, returned their waves, and thought about the seemingly never-ending reports that he needed to review. His parents were also away for the morning, out running errands, so it would be nice and quiet…a perfect environment to work.

As he walked back to the house, he turned and caught a fleeting glimpse of the disappearing horses and he stopped to watch until they were out of view. Despite their assurances of independence, he was always a little nervous when the girls went off alone, even though he knew they rode well and would be all right. He pushed his worries to the back of his mind and continued up the path to the house.

It was a rare treat to be back in New Mexico. When he and the girls were away, Marsh missed his parents' home, the Turquoise Trail Ranch, and he knew the girls did as well. Since they were five years old, Diane and Robin had spent their lives living in deep space, on whichever spaceship he was assigned. Two years ago, he had been promoted to captain and stationed aboard the Polaris, the newest, most advanced starship and the flagship of the fleet, making him the youngest person to ever command a starship. It also made him the only commander to have his own children aboard.

Space Central allowed crewmembers to bring immediate family along, but felt that commanders needed to devote one hundred percent of their concentration to command duties and were, therefore, prohibited from bringing their families. That rule had held until he was given command of the Polaris. It was the position he had spent his career working toward, but he would not accept unless his daughters could live with him. "The only way I can give my complete attention to my command duties," he argued vehemently to his superiors at Space Central, "is if I know my children are safe with me." There wasn't much of a debate at headquarters. When the Polaris was first commissioned, it was done so with Marsh in mind, and he was the only one ever considered to sit at her helm. And since none of the other commanders were married or had children, Space Central changed the policy to accommodate him and his daughters.

A deep sigh of contentment escaped as Marsh thought of his girls. For a man who never expected to have children, he could barely remember a time without them. Their entrance into his life had been sudden and bittersweet, but he never regretted a second of the life fate had handed him.

Diane and Robin were actually his nieces, the children of his oldest brother, Daniel. When the girls were infants, Diane eight-months old and Robin, a newborn, Daniel and his wife, Beth, were killed during an interplanetary war. Marsh, to his surprise, honor, and delight, had been named the girls' legal guardian. He loved and cherished them as if they were his own, and he was the only parent they had ever known. The life he had given them was unconventional, but they were adventurous—a Marsh family trait—and they loved every minute of it.

"Too bad Dad couldn't come," Robin said wistfully to her older sister. "We've barely spent any time with him."

"Yeah. If he had come it would have saved him from giving us all those instructions! Oh, and thanks," she added chuckling. "I know you saved me from saying something really stupid. You're very good at that!"

"I try, but one of these days…"

"I know, Rob. I know. I just get so frustrated when he treats us like little kids," Diane complained, but then admitted sheepishly, "To tell the truth, I wish he could have come too. He really is a lot of fun!" She glanced lovingly at her horse and added, "At least we have Pepper and Cloud to keep us company! I miss them so much when we're on the ship." Pepper swung his head at the mention of his name, and Diane leaned forward to kiss his neck.

Robin laughed. "We need to think of a way to convince Dad to let Pepper and Cloud aboard the Polaris. The ship sure is big enough!"

Images of their horses trotting though the corridors of a starship made Diane giggle. "Are you kidding? He won't even let us have a kitten!" she reminded her sister.

"'There will be no pets on the Polaris,'" Robin said, sitting up straight with a stern look on her face, imitating their father to a T, a skill she had perfected. That decree was a sore point with the sisters. Pets on a starship were at the captain's discretion. Marsh did not allow any and would not bend, even though his daughters were animal lovers and continually argued with him. But at least on the ranch they had their horses, the cats that roamed the stables, and a couple of dogs that the ranch hands kept.

A few years earlier, when they had outgrown the ponies they had been riding, Marsh had surprised his daughters with the horses. He had taken the girls to a horse show, observed which horses they liked, and then went back and procured both animals. The sisters had been ecstatic. Robin, who had fallen in love with the white horse because he had the most beautiful eyes she'd ever seen, promptly announced, "I'm naming my horse Cloud." Diane had looked at her horse carefully. He was gray with a black tail, mane, and socks. "I think his name should be Pepper," she said thoughtfully. It had been a good choice—he was spirited and the name suited him perfectly.

The girls had assumed their father would train Pepper and Cloud, and had been shocked when he announced that they had to do it themselves, with supervision from him or their grandparents'. "The bond between horse and rider begins with the training," he had told them. "If you train the horses yourselves, they will be loyal to you forever." The sisters had worked very hard that summer, and the result had been worth it—Pepper and Cloud loved the girls just as much as the girls loved their steeds.

Diane and Robin chatted casually as they made their way through the open fields that bordered the ranch, enjoying the scenic view of the mountains, a sight they missed living in space. Pepper and Cloud walked leisurely and stopped to munch on grass whenever they got a chance. It was a glorious March morning. The air was brisk, and the grass still sparkled with moisture from the previous evening's scheduled rainfall.

Programming the weather had been one of the greatest scientific achievements of the twenty-second century, and for the past one hundred years, weather-related disasters had almost ceased to exist. Plus, as an added benefit, outdoor events could be planned without fear of inclement weather, a boon to people everywhere!

Diane looked at Robin and smirked impishly. "Race you to the creek!" she shouted, and urged Pepper into a gallop before Robin could even answer.

"Hey, wait!" Robin yelled, taken by surprise, but Diane was already out of hearing range. "Not fair," she muttered, nudging Cloud to follow Pepper's lead.

Diane, unlike her sister, liked to ride fast and see the landscape whiz by. Robin preferred to take nature walks and enjoy the scenery and got annoyed with her sister's insistence on speed.

Knowing Robin wouldn't catch up, Diane slowed until her sister was alongside her. "Slowpoke," she teased with a grin.

"You cheat," Robin stated so seriously that Diane laughed at her sister's stern reprimand. Though Robin tried not to, she couldn't help herself and ended up laughing too.

"How about a compromise?" Diane proposed, hoping to appease her sister.

"What? A *slow* gallop?" Robin asked sarcastically.

The horses were walking at a nice, leisurely pace again and she was perfectly happy to keep it that way.

Diane was about to suggest a trot, but thought better of it. "Okay, you win," she said, and was gratified with her sister's smile. "We'll walk."

They rode slowly for a mile or so until they came to a fork in the road. Diane hesitated and looked to her right, where the terrain changed and the road became hilly and rocky.

Robin followed her sister's gaze. "Don't even think about it," she warned. "If we go up there and Dad finds out, he'll be furious and cancel the picnic tomorrow. I don't know about you, but we only have a few days of shore leave left, and I would rather be picnicking than sitting in my room staring at four walls."

"Yeah, me too," Diane reluctantly agreed, and turned her horse in the direction of the creek. "I hope he finishes his work today. A picnic would be fun—especially if he's in one of his exploring moods!"

"I know! Maybe he can find some more uncharted trails like he did last summer."

The trio had ventured up to the highest point in Santa Fe reachable on horseback. The sisters had been awestruck at the tranquil beauty surrounding them. From every angle, no matter which way they turned, there were mountains—high, regal peaks that refused to go unnoticed and unadmired.

"Would you mind if I asked Dad to find some trails that go past the old turquoise mines?" Robin asked. "I know we've done it before, but I love it."

"Sure. I like it too. You can collect rocks, and maybe I can find some nice stones to make beads from. And maybe," Diane added, her eyes brightening, "we can even convince him to camp out again!" It wouldn't take much persuading, she knew—he was always up for some exploring. After their adventure in the mountains, he had found them a secluded campground, and they spent the night under the stars.

It had become impossible for the sisters to think of the stars and not think of their father. When they were very little girls, before Marsh had taken them to live with him, and they still lived on the ranch with their grandparents, Diane and Robin would watch the sky every night. They wondered which planet he was on and when he was coming home. They would make up stories about how he was, at that very second, trying to find his way back to them. He never disappointed them. He always came home.

"Come on, Rob. We're almost at the creek. One last gallop!"

"No!"

"Canter?"

"No!"

"Trot? Please?"

Robin sighed. "Oh, all right! But a slow trot," she added, her green eyes blazing defiantly.

"A slow trot it is!" Diane yelled, victorious at last, and the two horses trotted side by side until they reached the creek.

Dismounting quickly and grabbing the binoculars

from her saddlebag, Robin yelled eagerly, "Let's go!" She loved to bird-watch and was always on the lookout for a new species she'd never seen.

Diane sighed and rolled her eyes. "Just a minute. Let me get my book," she said as she retrieved the latest novel she was reading from her saddlebag. She found bird-watching boring and wondered where Robin got the patience to wait around for hours while staring at the trees, but had to admit she was impressed with her sister's fortitude and knowledge. Sitting against a large elm tree whose leafy branches provided good shade, she opened her book and settled in to read.

A strange sound caught Robin's attention and she raised her binoculars to the sky. "Do you hear that low humming noise?" she asked while searching for the origin of the sound.

Startled by the strange hum, Diane jumped up. "What kind of bird is it?"

Robin continued to search the trees, adjusting her binoculars to get a clearer view. "It's not any bird I've ever heard." Then she spotted something. "Quick, take a look at that," she said excitedly as she pointed and handed the binoculars to Diane, who had come to stand next to her sister.

The hair on Diane's arms suddenly stood on end. "Oh, wow…what is it, Rob?"

"I…I…don't know. I've never seen anything like it."

Both girls pressed their palms to their ears as the humming sound grew louder and they stared at what looked like a tunnel of light that seemed to have no beginning or end. The light, similar to a spotlight, but brighter, intensified, and they had to shield their eyes from it.

"Run!" Diane screeched.

The girls sprinted out of the woods and toward their horses, but Pepper and Cloud had spooked and taken off as if running for their lives. *At least the horses are safe,* Diane thought when she saw the horses galloping away, and then wondered, *safe from what?* She didn't know, but her instincts told her that she and Robin were in imminent danger and she was helpless to stop it.

There was no escaping the light, which followed them wherever they moved and, within seconds, the sisters were completely enveloped in it.

"What's happening?" Robin cried. "Who's doing this?" Her thoughts flashed to the scheduled picnic and she wondered, in horror, if she and Diane would be alive to go. *Oh...where is Daddy?* she thought.

"I'm numb all over!" Diane yelled to her sister. Her instinct was to grab Robin's hand, but when she tried, she realized she was paralyzed where she stood. Robin didn't answer. A look in her direction showed that she, too, was rooted to the ground, the look of fear so profound on her face that Diane was sure it mimicked her own. Unable to move, but her mind racing, Diane remembered how, just an hour earlier, she had given her father a hard time when he wanted to help them. She'd give anything for his help now. *Oh...where is Daddy?* she thought.

Then, suddenly, the girls felt an intense wave of heat and the tingle of a transporter. As they passed out, Diane and Robin's last thoughts were of being ripped from the family they loved and the overwhelming fear they might never see them again.

CHAPTER 2

Trouble on the Polaris

Still thinking of his girls and grinning, Marsh climbed the porch steps and eyed the wicker rocking chairs that overlooked the corral and the beautiful view of the mountains. He considered relaxing in one, but he knew if he wanted to spend time with his daughters the next day, he would have to get through the work that awaited him. So he went inside instead and made his way to the office behind the living room that his mother had graciously offered to share with him while he was home.

At least here at the ranch he had a pleasant environment to work, much better than his cluttered office on the Polaris. Marsh sat at the desk and realized how incongruous it was. *Here I am*, he thought, *doing reports for the most modern starship in the galaxy on one of the oldest pieces of furniture on Earth.* The desk was one of his mother's antique 'finds,' an eighteenth-century roll-top that had taken her months to painstakingly refinish. Marsh shared his mother's love of antiques, and he sat back to admire the workmanship, both hers and that of the original craftsman.

Sitting at the old desk made Marsh realize how much he missed the ranch. The Polaris was his home now, and he went where the stars took him…and where Space Central sent him. But this big, old house held so many wonderful memories. His mother had insisted on this ranch. She had wanted an old-fashioned home to raise a family in—and that's exactly what she got.

Modern homes came equipped with everything from automated food dispensers that produced complete meals with a simple voice command, to self-cleaning rooms that immediately eradicated dirt and dust. But this old house didn't have any of those conveniences. It even had real doors, with doorknobs that had to be turned! The very same doors his daughter Diane loved to slam when she was angry! Marsh had to admit that sometimes, when he was in a rush, he'd bang into one, expecting it to open automatically for him.

An incoming subspace communication interrupted his thoughts. His mother, a communications expert who routinely did consulting work for Space Central, had the most advanced equipment available. Within seconds, a life-size hologram materialized in front of him. Gerroll, his second-in-command and a native from the planet Nimian, was sitting at his station with a concerned look on his face.

Normally, Marsh's first reaction upon seeing Gerroll was to smile. Not only was Gerroll a brilliant scientist, mathematician, and navigator, but he was also the one who kept the bridge crew laughing with his silly pranks and jokes. He had met Gerroll on one of his first assignments and had served with him numerous times over the years. Diane and Robin had known him since they were toddlers and absolutely adored him…and the feeling was mutual.

As all Nimians, Gerroll's hair was pure white, even though he was still a young man of thirty-seven. The thick, straight strands were pulled back and tied in a braid that reached halfway down his back. His eyes were doe-like—large, gentle, and soft brown. They radiated warmth and trust to all who looked into them.

The inhabitants of Nimian were telepaths—Gerroll could read minds—not individual thoughts, but images and perceptions. He rarely did, however, because he considered it an invasion of privacy to those around him. He was highly trained in the art of blocking out surrounding thoughts, and only in extreme emergencies would he use his inborn gift.

"Good morning, Captain. I hope I am not disturbing you." Gerroll's voice usually had a musical lilt to it, but he sounded serious this morning.

"Reports, Gerroll. I'm doing reports and I welcome the interruption. Is anything wrong?" Marsh questioned quickly, in reaction to Gerroll's expression and grave tone.

"We're not exactly sure, Sir, but I thought you should be apprised of the morning's events."

"What happened?" Marsh asked, alarmed, and immediately thought, *I should never have left the Polaris.* He ran his fingers in nervous anticipation through his thick, dark, wavy hair, as he waited for Gerroll's response.

"Earlier this morning, the ship was scanned by an exceptionally strong, sophisticated probe, unlike any I have ever encountered."

"Do you have any idea what it was scanning for?" Marsh inquired, his concern growing by the second. He stood up and began to pace the room, all thoughts of the reports forgotten.

"No, Captain, but the object of the search obviously wasn't found because there has been no contact since."

Marsh stopped pacing and considered this for a second, then asked, "Any adverse effects?"

"Yes, that is why I wanted to contact you, but I had to wait until the communication station was repaired. It seems the probe has burnt our main control panels. We have impulse power only, and we are operating on emergency life-support systems."

"How long until the repairs are completed?"

"Lieutenant Wells has estimated a minimum of two days."

"Tell her that I want all repairs completed by tomorrow at the latest." He hated to put Kate Wells, the ship's chief engineer, under such pressure, but he didn't like the fact that his ship was operating in any way less than perfect. He could see her brown eyes deep in concentration as she worked to keep her engine room running smoothly. Her curly, dark red hair was always in disarray and, although she tried to keep it tucked into a bun, silky wisps were forever falling out. She'd simply brush them off her face and continue working.

"Was anybody hurt?" Marsh asked, and prayed for a negative response.

"No, Captain, which is fortunate since Dr. Wells is stuck on the planet Saras. The transporter is also non-operational."

"Are there any ships in your vicinity that might be responsible for the probe?" He longed to be sitting in his command chair, seeing for himself instead of getting answers after the fact.

"None that we can detect, Captain."

"Keep scanning the area."

"Yes, Sir."

"Gerroll, patch me through to Dr. Wells. I want to know how his mission is progressing."

"Yes, Captain. Just give me a second to make the connection."

Gerroll's hologram faded and within seconds, Dr. Matthew Wells appeared, standing in a medical facility surrounded by patients. Marsh acknowledged his friend with a nod and waited as Matt finished giving an injection to a frightened child, who calmed visibly under the doctor's care. The doctor was six foot three, a couple of inches taller than Marsh, muscular and well-built with a perfectly trimmed goatee and mustache, a bald head, rich gleaming mahogany skin and a bedside manner that put his patients at ease and made them feel safe, protected, and cared for. Without question, they were in the best medical hands Space Central had to offer.

Marsh had first met Matt when they were in the third grade and had become best friends, bonding immediately over their shared love of outer space and the desire to someday live on a starship. Matt wanted to be a doctor on one and Marsh, of course, wanted to command one. They entered the Intergalactic Academy of Space Studies at the same time and, even after graduation, had kept in close contact. When Marsh took command of the Polaris, Matt Wells had been his first and only choice for chief medical officer.

"I won't keep you…I see you are busy. How's the assignment going?"

Dr. Wells was currently on Saras, helping the Sarasians control an epidemic of Barulian Fever, a virus that killed its victims within forty-eight hours if not treated. The Sarasian ambassador, Jonathan Kaner, had requested Dr. Wells's presence personally, having worked with him a few years before, during a similar outbreak. The League of Universal Planets, an Intergalactic United Nations, of which Space Central was the military division, had been eager to please this fairly new member planet because of its strategic position as a much-needed space dock, so they immediately agreed to the ambassador's request.

"Everything's going fine here, Captain," Matt said with a hint of a smile. He couldn't help the smile—it always appeared when he called his boyhood friend by his formal title. "It will only be another few days, and then we will have this epidemic under control."

Marsh returned the smile. "Glad to hear it."

Matt's smile faded. "I heard the Polaris had a rough morning."

"Seems so. Looks like Kate will have her hands full in the engine room for the next few days."

"Katie can handle it!" Matt said, his face beaming as he spoke of his wife. "Too bad the girls aren't aboard, though, to keep Jared company. It was perfect timing for you and the girls to take some shore leave, but he must be lonely with them gone and Katie and me so busy." Kate and Matt's son, Jared, was the same age as Diane and Robin, and the three were usually inseparable.

"He'll see them sooner than expected," Marsh said. "We were scheduled to return next week, but now we'll leave as soon as possible. Keep up the good work, Matt, and please send my regards to Ambassador Kaner. Marsh out."

When the connection with Wells was broken, Marsh was reconnected with the Polaris.

"Gerroll, keep me updated on all repairs."

"I will, Captain."

"Good. I'll speak with you later. Marsh out."

There was no way he could return to his reports now. He walked outside into the late-morning sunshine and felt the frustration wash over him. He paced back and forth in the front yard, kicking the sand as he walked. Pacing helped him think and calm him. *I should be on my ship with my crew,* he thought, even though he knew Gerroll could handle the situation. The men and women on the Polaris were his responsibility and their safety was his utmost concern. His loyalty to his crew was matched only by their loyalty to him. Now, he was down here and they were up there, and all he could do was wait for Gerroll to contact him with updates.

CHAPTER 3

THE SEARCH

Sarah Marsh leaned against the kitchen counter, her worried brown eyes glued to her son and her fair hair a mess from nervously running her fingers through it. "Where could they be?"

She and her husband, Jake, had returned home more than an hour ago. Lunch was ready and had been on the table for over half an hour, and the girls still weren't back from their morning ride. More troubling was that all attempts to reach them had been in vain. Sarah looked back and forth from her husband to her son, who were standing together across from her. She was amazed, as always, at the resemblance between them, both with thick, dark, wavy hair (her husband's now graying), and sparkling green eyes.

"I don't know, Mom. I told them to be home in time for lunch," Marsh replied, glancing at the table that was set with the girls' favorite foods, not sure if he should be worried or angry. "I'll try reaching them again." He tapped his communication badge and tried one more time to contact his daughters, but got no response.

"Maybe they took a hike and left their stuff in the saddlebags," Jake suggested. "That would explain why they're not answering." *Or, they found themselves in some mischief again!* he thought.

"Bill, why don't you go see if you can find them?" Sarah said, eager to see her grandchildren home safely.

Marsh hadn't heard from Gerroll, either, and although he was sure there was probably nothing new to report, he was anxious for information. He couldn't sit still any longer. He needed to do something.

"Okay, Mom. Good idea." Marsh turned to his father. "Come on, Dad. Let's take a drive and see if we can find them. We'll take the hovercar. It's faster than horseback, and if you drive, I can scan the ground and look for them." He couldn't help but notice the look of relief on his mother's face, and he could no longer ignore the feeling he was getting in the pit of his stomach—a feeling he had learned long ago never to ignore, because it was one of his best barometers for impending trouble.

The hovercar, which flies about fifty feet above the ground, covered the distance quickly. About a mile from the creek, Marsh spotted the horses running wildly through the fields.

"Look, Dad, over there! Pepper and Cloud!" Marsh yelled. "Put down as close as you can."

They leaped out of the car and tried to round up the horses, but the animals wouldn't allow the men anywhere near them. Both Pepper and Cloud shied nervously. Something had definitely spooked them. It took awhile and a lot of soft talking, but they were finally able to get close enough to grab the horses' reins.

"Shhh, it's okay, boy," Marsh cooed as he stroked Cloud's neck. "What happened, huh?" If only Cloud could tell them. He checked the saddlebag. "Robin's communication badge and her snacks and water are still in here," he reported to his father.

Jake found the same in Pepper's saddlebag and felt a chill run down his spine.

"Quick, Dad. Let's get to the creek. The horses will find their way back to the barn," Marsh said as he gave a quick slap on Cloud's rump to get the animal moving. The men quickly got back into the hovercar.

As they approached the creek, they couldn't believe what they saw. A ring of singed grass covered the entire area.

"Put her down, Dad. Quickly!" the younger Marsh shouted urgently, and they jumped out of the car as soon as it touched ground.

"Let's split up," Marsh called to his father as he ran into the brush. His military training ingrained, he covered ground quickly, his experienced eyes taking in every detail. He knew exactly which way to go. He'd been here often with Diane and Robin, and they usually followed the same path. Hopefully, this wasn't the one time the girls deviated from their usual course. He pushed branches and brush out of his way as he ran. They radiated a curious heat as he tried to keep them from scraping his body. *What could have done this?* He would give anything for the diagnostic instruments and computer on the Polaris.

Something caught his eye and he stopped short. He bent down, brushed away the dirt, and picked up Robin's binoculars. And not more than five feet away was Diane's book, the pages singed from the heat. His stomach tightened, and he was suddenly aware of his heart pounding in his chest. Fear gripped his entire being. He didn't believe in coincidences and immediately thought of the probe that had burnt out the controls on his ship.

As his mind collated all the details, it hit him—his daughters had been abducted. He did not know by whom, but he did know one thing…they were definitely hostile.

Marsh never panicked—a starship captain couldn't panic—but this was the closest he had ever come. He had no choice but to remain calmly efficient so he could do what needed to be done.

His mother, however, uncharacteristically panicked enough for all of them. Sarah Marsh was always cool, calm, and collected, and she handled emergencies with detailed efficiency—raising three adventurous sons had perfected those traits—but the abduction of her granddaughters was something entirely different.

The first thing Marsh did after breaking the news to her was contact Gerroll.

"I agree with your hypothesis, Captain. The coincidence is too great."

"Gerroll, I need computer readings from the area around the creek to match with your readings of the probe. We have to be certain it was the same probe that scanned both the Polaris and here. I need the Polaris, Gerroll, and I need her now. How are the repairs progressing?"

"Life-support systems are all back on line and the transporter is functioning, but Lieutenant Wells has informed me that the engines will not achieve full power until late tomorrow. At this time we have impulse power only."

"Not good enough," Marsh said impatiently. "I can't wait that long." He paused only for a second. "I have an idea, though. I will be in contact with you soon. Marsh out."

After ending his conversation with Gerroll, Marsh instructed the computer to connect him with his desired destination. The connection was almost instantaneous.

"Space Central Main Headquarters. This is Ensign Willis. How may I help you?" asked the young brunette manning the communication station.

"I'd like to talk with Admiral Packard. Please tell her it's Captain William Marsh."

Ensign Willis was still a cadet at the Intergalactic

Academy of Space Studies and couldn't believe her luck—she'd heard so much about the famous Captain Marsh, and now here she was…face to face with him… at least on the viewscreen. She smiled sweetly and had to admit that he really was as handsome as the Academy gossip rumored…*his dark, wavy hair and sparkling green eyes are striking, but it's his boyish grin that makes him irresistible,* other cadets had said. But there was no sign of that grin right now.

Normally, Marsh would have taken the time to chat with Ensign Willis, but not today. He remained stone-faced, his mind focused on his task, and his thoughts only of his daughters.

"One moment please, Captain," she said, disappointed that he wasn't more talkative.

Marsh stared impatiently at the Space Central insignia, a cluster of stars nestled in a cloud, the same icon as on their communication badges, while he waited to be connected to Admiral Packard. Instead, Ensign Willis returned.

"I'm sorry, Captain. The Admiral is in a meeting."

"Interrupt her. Tell her it's urgent," he barked, then softened his tone and added, "Please." He tried to smile, but it didn't come easily. "It is very important."

"I'll try, Captain, but she left instructions not to be disturbed."

"Thank you, Ensign."

The Space Central insignia again. This time it remained on the screen longer, but Marsh was finally rewarded with the admiral's appearance. Her salt and pepper hair was short and stylish, and her eyes were a piercing blue.

"Admiral Packard here. What's the emergency, Captain Marsh?"

"I'm sorry to pull you out of a meeting, Admiral, but I need your help immediately."

"I gathered that, Captain. I thought you were on shore leave. What's the problem?"

"The Polaris was scanned this morning by what my second-in-command says was a very sophisticated probe that burnt out the main engines and incapacitated most of the systems on the ship. There was no indication of what it was searching for, and there were no signs of any ships in the area."

Marsh took a deep breath and continued the explanation that still seemed impossible to believe. "Then, about an hour or so ago, Diane and Robin appear to have been abducted while out horseback riding. The area where they were has been burnt by what I believe is the same probe that scanned the Polaris."

Packard was shocked. "The Polaris damaged? Your girls abducted? By whom? Why?" She shot out the questions one by one, like bullets, concern rich in her voice.

"I don't know, Admiral," Marsh replied, shaking his head. "But I need your help to find out."

"What do you need, Captain?"

"The repairs on the Polaris will take a few days to complete. Plus, Dr. Wells is still working on Saras and needs the ship for supplies and the computer. I need diagnostic instruments to gather information to feed into the Polaris's computer, and I need a shuttlecraft to get back to her."

Packard didn't hesitate. "That's no problem. We can have both to you this afternoon."

Marsh exhaled, not realizing that he had been holding his breath while waiting for the Admiral's response. "Thank you, Admiral. I appreciate your help."

"Is there anything else?" Packard asked.

"A few prayers would be nice."

Packard smiled, that request being an easy one. "You've got those without asking. It sounds as if your problem is both official and personal. Keep me informed of your progress."

"I will, Admiral."

"Good. Packard out."

Admiral Packard was true to her word, although it wasn't as quick as Marsh would have preferred. It took more than three hours before a shuttlecraft was delivered to him, and Marsh spent every second pacing. But Admiral Packard had the foresight to send two shuttlecrafts, so Marsh wouldn't have to waste any time returning the pilot to Houston—Space Central's main headquarters.

Marsh went back to where the girls had been abducted and took several readings. Then he returned to the house to say goodbye to his parents.

"I'll find them, Mom," he promised. "I will bring them home."

Marsh hugged her, and then it was her turn to reassure him. "I know you will, Bill." But her voice wasn't as confident as her words.

Jake pulled his son in close for a hug and a few encouraging pats on the back. There was no need for words because they understood each other, their unspoken thoughts the same. *Bring the girls home. Take care of Mom. Everything will be okay!*

CHAPTER 4

THE ALIEN SHIP

"Ohhhhh," Robin groaned. She opened her eyes and then instantly closed them to shut out the light. "My head is killing me."

Diane stirred on the bed next to her and tried to sit up. "Oh, mine too," she moaned and lay back down like a limp rag doll. "What happened? Where are we?" She reached for her communication badge, but it was gone…where it went and who took it, she didn't know.

"The last thing I remember," Robin said very softly, not wanting to make her headache any worse, "is the bright light at the creek, feeling hot, and then the tingle of a transporter."

"Yeah, that's what I remember also," Diane agreed, then paused to choke down the sickening feeling rising in her throat. "I'd give anything for one of Dr. Wells's pills. I swear, my head feels like it's in a vice." She held her aching head with both hands in an effort to dull the pain, but it didn't help.

Neither girl moved. They tried to lie as still as possible, waiting for the pain to subside. After a few long minutes of silence, Diane asked apprehensively, "How…how long have we been here?"

Robin squinted in agony when she tried to read her watch display. "I'm not sure. It's 0800 hours now. We were at the creek yesterday at…let me think… everything's still a blur… at 0900 hours. That would mean we've been out," she calculated through the haze, "almost a whole day. That's assuming it *was* yesterday and not the day before or some other day. We don't know how long we've been out." She closed her eyes, exhausted.

Diane tried to sit up again, this time very gingerly. "I remember seeing the horses take off. Daddy must have found them by now and is looking for us," she said, trying to sound as confident as she could under the circumstances.

"Hope he knows more than we do," Robin said flatly as she, too, attempted a sitting position. "Can you stand?"

"Don't push me…I can barely sit," Diane replied, remaining very still with her eyes closed. She took a deep, shaky breath.

Robin stood up unsteadily while holding the nearest wall for support. She wondered if her legs could really have turned to rubber.

Diane finally attempted to stand, getting up slowly

on her wobbly feet. She leaned against the wall, then turned and rested her cheek on it so she could feel its coolness. *An ice pack would be nice about now*, she thought. *So would a familiar face.* But she didn't think either would materialize anytime soon.

They were standing in a small rectangular room completely made of glass. Actually, three of the four walls were glass. There was nothing where the fourth wall should be, and the girls assumed it was a force field. The missing fourth wall faced a long, empty, gray corridor. The only objects in the room were the two small beds they had been in, which were attached directly to the wall; a little, round, black table that was bolted to the floor; and a small, closed-off room in the corner.

"What is this place?" Robin asked, looking around.

"It…it looks like a childcare center of some sort."

From where they stood, they could see through to at least a dozen similar rooms, one right next to the other. All of the rooms had what appeared to be three or four cribs in them. No decoration or anything that suggested warmth. Just cold, sterile, glass rooms with cribs. But no babies. In fact, no other people at all. The sisters were very much alone in this cold, desolate prison.

Robin sat back down on the bed, horrified, and Diane sat down next to her. She rested her still-aching head on her sister's shoulder.

"Why?" Diane asked, her voice trembling and her eyes stinging with tears, "Why are we here?"

Robin didn't respond, but Diane could feel her

sister shrug. She looked over and saw tears rolling down Robin's cheeks. They sat silently for a few minutes, both contemplating the events that had put them in this predicament.

"Well, aside from these rotten headaches, we seem to be okay," Diane said, trying hard to compose herself. She got up, went back to her own bed and sat up against the wall. "I…I guess for now we have no choice but to wait and see what happens. Something's *got* to happen eventually. Right?"

"Yeah, and then maybe we can figure out why we're here," Robin agreed. "And besides," she added brightly, "Dad will probably show up and get us out of here. I'm sure he will." Then she added tentatively, "Aren't you?"

"Without a question," Diane answered with false bravado. Then she joked to lighten their mood, "Unless he orchestrated this whole thing to get a few days of peace and quiet!"

Despite her growing fear and ever-present headache, Robin laughed. "Hey, you never know! He keeps threatening to throw us into the brig if we don't start behaving. Maybe this is just one of his 'creative' lessons!"

Diane chuckled at the thought. "Well, if it is, it's working. And if it's not, let's not give him any ideas!"

They sat in silence again, neither knowing what else they could say or do to change the situation. Finally, they got up to do another inspection of the missing fourth wall. They both stood and stared at it.

"Think the force field is activated?" Robin asked.

"Um… yeah! It would be nice if we were free to

walk out of here, Rob, but somehow…I don't think so. But be my guest…try it," Diane said and ceremoniously extended her hand as an invitation, and quickly moved out of the way.

Robin looked at her sister and then at the blank space where the wall should be. She put her finger out to touch the space, and then pulled it back. Hesitantly, she put her finger back up. *One, two, three*, she silently counted to herself, and on the count of three, she quickly touched the empty space with the tip of her finger. The whole area sparked and crackled, and both girls were thrown back, losing their balance and tumbling to the floor.

"Guess what, Rob," Diane asked as she hit the hard surface.

"What?"

"It's activated! Are you okay?"

"Yeah, fine," Robin told her, but was sucking on her injured finger.

Both girls remained on the floor for a while, looking around.

"What do you think is in there?" Robin asked apprehensively, indicating the small room in the corner.

"Beats me. A closet probably. You tested the force field. I guess it's my turn to be the brave one," Diane stated boldly, even though she didn't move for a minute. She finally got up and stood near the door of the tiny room, but far enough away so the door wouldn't sense her presence and slide open.

"Well, open it already!"

"I will. I will. I'm just being cautious," Diane said, but she was petrified of what might be on the other side. "Give me a minute." She swallowed hard, wiped her hands on her pants, held her breath, and moved directly in front of the small door. It slid open quietly. She hesitated just a second, and then quickly poked her head into the open doorway.

"IT'S A BATHROOM!"

Robin smiled. "Thank heavens!"

Diane sighed in relief.

Robin got up, walked past her sister and into the bathroom. "Come here. You've got to see these," she yelled as she held up two long tunic robes, one green and the other red, both made of a soft, shimmery material and lined with silver-braided piping. She had found them, folded neatly, inside a small closet in the bathroom.

"I wonder if they are for us," Diane mused. "They're so pretty!" She took the red one, her favorite color, and held it up for closer inspection.

Robin berated her sister. "You're not supposed to like prison garb, Diane."

"Yeah, well, it's better than wearing stripes and certainly more flattering!" Diane joked, holding the tunic against her body as one might hold a beautiful ball gown so her sister could inspect it.

Robin laughed at Diane's attempt to take a few dance steps while holding the robe in front of her. "I still think we better remain in our own clothes for now. Hopefully—"

Diane cut her short and pointed toward a small opening in the force field. "Uh, oh," she whispered. "I think we've got company."

Robin turned and her mouth fell open. Standing there, about to enter, was the biggest 'person' she had ever seen. He stood at least seven feet tall, maybe more, with features that were oversized, even for his huge frame. He was wearing one of those long tunic robes—his in a metallic gold, which matched his large, bulging eyes that seemed to glow with a sinister radiance. His dark hair was pulled tightly from his head and tied in a knot that sat on the back of his neck, which accented the evil scowl that seemed permanently etched upon his face. He was carrying a tray that looked small in his huge hands. It had two bowls and two glasses of, hopefully, water.

"He can be *your* date!" Diane whispered as he approached them. "I think I'll sit this one out." For every step he took toward them, the sisters took one step back until they hit the wall.

"Nourishment," he said as he lumbered in their direction. His voice was deep but colorless, probably an intergalactic translator, which translated universal concepts into all languages. He placed some kind of gross-looking brown soup on the table and left as quickly as he came, not talking to them or even looking in their direction, leaving them pinned to the wall and afraid to move. They had been too frightened to do anything but stare at him and, after he left, it took a few minutes before they moved from the safety of the wall.

"I…I think I want to go home, now," Robin whined as she moved over to the table to inspect what he had put down.

"You *think* you want to go home?"

"Actually, I'm quite sure about it," Robin confirmed. "Diane, we've got to find out what's going on here." Her whole body felt icy and she shivered uncontrollably. She was shaking from a place so deep inside that she couldn't determine where it started. "I'm so scared."

They sat down on the floor next to the table and brought the tray down with them. It appeared the glasses did have water in them, and the girls drank them immediately, quenching their growing thirst. Then they turned their attention to the bowls. Robin picked up her spoon, filled it and turned it on its side, letting the brown liquid, which looked like watery mud, drip back into the bowl. She did this a few times as Diane watched.

"I'm scared, too," Diane said, "but, as Dad taught us…survival first. We'd better eat something. I guess we should try the soup." She stared at it dubiously and then looked at Robin. "What if it's poisoned?"

"If they wanted to kill us, they would have done it already."

"That's true," Diane conceded and continued to stare at the bowl.

Robin gingerly sipped some of the soup off the spoon. "Euuuuu! This is viler than vile!" she cried and spit it out.

"In which case, I'll pass. Maybe lunch will be better."

"Can't get much worse," Robin said in disgust. She pushed the tray into the corner of the room, and they never gave it a second glance.

"I wonder where they're taking us," Diane mused.

The girls knew they were on a spaceship. Years of space travel had given them the feel of a moving vessel. They could sense the silent engines.

"And who 'they' are," Robin added.

CHAPTER 5

DESPICABLE

The Mog's home planet was on the other side of the Frazon boundary line, which the League of Universal Planets, the LUP, considered enemy space, because it was occupied by the LUP's sworn enemies, the Frazons. By a mutual agreement put in place over seventy-five years ago, both parties agreed to stay on their side of the boundary line. Crossing by either party could be considered a declaration of war and, for the most part, both the Frazons and the LUP had stayed on their respective sides. There had been a few skirmishes over the years, the last one involving the Polaris, but nothing that had led to a full-blown war between the Frazons and the LUP… at least not yet.

The Frazons' entire culture was based on the conquering and subsequent rule of others, and there were many planets on the Frazon side of the boundary line where the inhabitants were conquered captives under

Frazon rule. As long as the people followed the laws set down by their Frazon governors, they were free to live their lives as normal—as normal as one can live under Frazon rule, that is.

The Mog were one such conquered people. They didn't like the Frazons, but had learned to coexist peacefully. Not that they had much of a choice; it was coexist or die.

The Mog captain, Commander Blassen, sat ramrod straight in his command chair in the center of the bridge. He was an imposing man with a mean temper. His gold eyes, which were characteristic of the Mog, would blaze, and the veins on his neck and forehead bulge when he didn't get the answers he wanted. His mood could turn as black as his hair, which he wore in a long ponytail. More than one crewmember had felt Blassen's wrath, and they tended to stand out of striking distance when they answered his questions.

It was not a large bridge, but then again, it was not a large ship. Blassen had only twelve crewmembers and they obeyed him without question because he had saved each one of them from a very nasty fate.

Blassen chose carefully those who served with him. He needed military men who had experience on spaceships, so he turned to the Mog's highly respected Space Fleet for his candidates—an easy course of action, as he was an ex-Space Fleet commander himself.

Blassen had actually been one of the highest ranking and most experienced commanders in the fleet when he decided the job didn't sufficiently compensate him. During a routine mission, he had stumbled upon a way to bring himself great wealth. It wasn't legal—it wasn't even moral—but kidnapping children had allowed him to live very nicely.

He preferred to abduct infants because they were in greater demand and gave him less trouble, but this time he had made an exception. Luckily for him, child abduction was not a popular craft these days, and he was just about the only person one could turn to if they were in the market to capture one of those noisy, screaming, constantly wet creatures. Since he was not a Frazon, he was free to cross the boundary line, without being pestered by worrying planets.

He didn't like children, never had, and it amazed him that he had actually been one himself—or that anyone would really desire one. He couldn't blame his parents for abandoning him.

Blassen resigned from the Space Fleet with a chest full of military medals and then, for all intents and purposes, disappeared. No one knew where he was or what he did. No one, that is, except those who hired him. He was quite well known among the merchants of the black market.

He had secured a science vessel and had it refitted to his specifications, programmed the computer himself to do what he needed it to do, and then went in search of crewmembers. He covertly rescued Space Fleet members who had been convicted of treasonous crimes and sentenced to labor camps for the remainder of their lives, thus ensuring their loyalty.

That was after confirming that they possessed—as he and all of the children he abducted did—one unique trait.

CHAPTER 6

PEANUT BUTTER AND PIZZA

Diane and Robin tried to cover their growing fears with small talk and humor, and encouraged each other to remain calm. Through the tears that did emerge, they consoled one another with the fact that their father would find them.

Lunch arrived via the same silent waiter. "Nourishment," he said as he put the bowls down, picked up the full breakfast bowls, and left, not even giving them a chance to speak.

"Extensive vocabulary he has," Robin observed.

Diane grinned. "Yeah, and the problem is, we've *got* to get some information out of him."

"I know. But he's so scary looking, I'm afraid to open my mouth," Robin admitted, shuddering at the thought of him. "We'll try again later. Let's see what's for lunch," she said, peering skeptically into the bowl.

It didn't look any more appetizing than breakfast. This time the bowls were filled with a thick, pasty, white cereal that tasted almost as bad as the soup.

"Do these people really eat this stuff or is it their equivalent of bread and water?" Robin pondered.

"Bread and water is at least palatable…this isn't," Diane said, playing with the gruel in her bowl, moving it around and around as if it would miraculously turn into something appetizing. Unfortunately, it didn't.

They each had a little, but only because they were so hungry. As they pushed the still-full bowls away, Robin asked, "Do you know what I would like?"

Diane got up from the floor and moved to the relative comfort of the bed. "No, tell me…what would you like?"

Robin remained seated on the floor. She wrapped her arms around her knees, looked up at her sister and, in a dreamy voice, drawing out each word, answered, "A thick, gooey, peanut butter sandwich with grape jelly and—"

"Raspberry," Diane interjected because she didn't like grape jelly. "Or strawberry."

"Okay, okay…you can have raspberry or strawberry jam. I want grape jelly and…marshmallow spread!"

"Yuk, Robin. I don't know how you eat that stuff. It ruins the taste of the peanut butter."

"I like it! This is my fantasy, and I can have whatever I want! Or, instead of peanut butter we could have…"

"Now you're talking!" Diane exclaimed. She knew exactly what her sister was thinking…

"Captain, we just received a message from Space Central," said Communications Officer Helen Diska.

"What does it say, Lieutenant?"

"Well, Sir, it says that…um…there are reports of numerous, unauthorized distress calls coming from the Polaris."

"Distress calls, Lieutenant? We haven't sent any distress calls. What kind of distress calls?"

"Calls for emergency deliveries, Sir, and they said to remind you that the unauthorized use of a distress signal is against Space Central regulations."

"I'm well aware of that, Lieutenant, but we haven't sent any distress calls—for emergency deliveries or anything else. Gerroll, are there any other ships in the area that might be in trouble?"

"No, Captain. We are the only ship in this sector."

"Lieutenant, what is the nature of the emergency? What are the requests for?"

Lieutenant Diska stared at her commanding officer, unable to respond.

"Lieutenant, I asked what the requests were for."

"Oh, no," Helen thought. "How am I going to tell him?"

"LIEUTENANT!" Marsh said, rather loudly, interrupting her thoughts and giving her no choice but to answer.

"Pizza pies, Sir," Diska spat out as quickly as she could.

His eyes widened and he swiveled in his chair to stare at her as if he could not believe he heard correctly. "Repeat that," he commanded.

She swallowed hard and said softly, "Pizza pies, Sir."

The bridge was silent. No one dared move or look at one another, except for Gerroll, who didn't even attempt to hide his amusement. Marsh slammed his hand down on the arm of his command chair, jumped up, and headed for the hyperlift.

Lieutenant Diska thought, as Marsh passed, that she wouldn't want to be on the receiving end of his wrath.

"Deck 17," Marsh said to the computerized hyperlift, the high-powered elevator that could take him anywhere, vertically or horizontally, on the ship. He leaned against the wall and thought about his daughters' latest prank. They must have accessed communications from the Secondary Control Room.

It started as an inaudible chuckle and by the time the doors slid open, he was laughing aloud. He changed directions and headed for the ship's kitchen instead.

For dinner that night they all had pizza, even Gerroll, who agreed that it was quite tasty. When the last piece was gone and they had finished licking their fingers, Marsh looked at his girls and said with his finger wagging, "No more distress calls, understand?"

Well fed, content, and very pleased with themselves, Diane and Robin nodded and smiled.

"Oh, and also," he added, "you can both spend the rest of the evening in your quarters."

The thought of pizza kept Diane and Robin's minds off their hunger for a little while, but the time went slowly, so they napped to help pass the day. When they awoke, it was almost dinnertime and by now they were absolutely starving. At the sound of footsteps, they turned to their silent butler…and dinner.

"Here he is again. This time we've got to try and talk to him," Diane said adamantly. Both girls rose to their feet to rally their courage in anticipation of a confrontation.

"Nourishment," he said in his usual monotone voice, and placed the tray on the small table.

"Is that all he knows how to say?" Robin whispered.

"I don't know. Let's ask him." Diane stood up tall and squared her shoulders, trying to look as brave and confident as she could. "Excuse me, Sir. Do you have a name?" she asked in her sweetest voice.

She was ignored. He didn't look at them, just carried on with his regular routine of taking away the old tray and putting down the new one.

"You try," Diane whispered to her sister. "Maybe you'll have better luck."

Robin edged a little closer and threw a barrage of questions at him, "Where are we? Why are we here? Who are you?" But she got absolutely no response. Finally, in frustration, she yelled, "Heelloooo, is anybody home?" She would have knocked on his head but there was no chance of reaching it as he stood over two feet taller than her.

He ignored the girls and their questions and once again left as quickly and quietly as he came. All the bravado in the world couldn't help their moods. Fear and apprehension took their appetites, but they picked at the food, anyway, to silence the rumbling in their stomachs.

Scared and alone, except for each other, they tried to sleep, painfully aware that for the first time, no one would be in to say good night.

CHAPTER 7

CAN YOU FINGER DANCE?

Rusus crossed the small bridge and stood next to his commander. "Commander Blassen, we have crossed the boundary line and are now back in Frazon space. It will not be long until we can deliver the girls to General Malon."

"We will not be delivering them to him, Rusus. I have other plans for them," Blassen replied, not even looking at his officer.

"Commander? I don't understand. I thought we were paid in advance for their abduction by the great Frazon Imperial Governor himself, General Malon."

Blassen sighed and explained, as he continued to watch the viewscreen in front of him, "The general seeks revenge against Marsh for his son's death during the last Frazon battle with the LUP. It was during a battle with Marsh that a Frazon warship was destroyed, and General

Malon's son along with it. The general wants Marsh's daughters in exchange for his son's life." Then with a wave of his hand he noted, "The general wants to execute the girls himself!" He looked at Rusus and continued the explanation. "But the general has not paid in currency, but in Frazon technology. As you know, I convinced him that dealing with Marsh would not be easy, and we would need the Frazon technology for camouflaging spaceships in order to achieve our goal. General Malon never argued. He immediately gave us the information we needed.

"And now, the general does not know we have the girls. When he contacted me, I told him that we had been unsuccessful in locating them. After all, it is common knowledge that Marsh keeps them well protected."

"But not from our probe, Commander," Rusus argued.

"Our probe is only good if we know where to look, and that is what I told the general. Since the girls were not on the Polaris as the general originally expected them to be, he told me to keep looking. I told him I would, but I can get an excellent price for them elsewhere. I didn't think it was necessary to tell the general that I tracked the girls to Marsh's home on Earth."

"You lied to General Malon? That is very risky, Commander," Rusus stated, trying to keep the alarm he felt out of his voice. He didn't want Blassen to think he didn't trust the decision. Instead, he decided to pursue something else Blassen had mentioned. "You said you could sell the girls elsewhere?"

"Yes, Rusus, where the general will *never* find them." Blassen smiled a conspiratorial smile at his officer.

"I do understand, Commander," Rusus said and returned the smile. "Is it possible?"

"Yes, I ran them through our computers, and they are perfect candidates, although I really didn't have to check. Marsh is very popular *everywhere,* and I already knew the answer."

"How lucky for us," Rusus said and laughed. "But double-crossing General Malon could be very dangerous," he added.

"Yes, you are right on both accounts, Rusus. I will tell the general that the girls were killed while being abducted. He'll never have a way to disprove it, and if he checks into Marsh's affairs, he will find that the girls vanished and were never heard from again. General Malon will have his revenge without ever having the girls, and I can, in essence, sell them twice—once for Frazon technology and again for a very large sum of space credits.

"We should cross through the portal tomorrow evening. Once we are on the other side, the general cannot find us. We will head back into LUP space where I have a perfect buyer in mind. A horrid man actually, even by our standards." Blassen laughed evilly and continued. "He lives on the godforsaken, isolated planet of Jastar and claims that he is in need of 'serving girls,' or so he calls them. Whatever, that's his affair. He's quite rich and will pay handsomely for them. We should reach our destination within thirty-six hours."

"Is it not too risky being in LUP space with the

girls aboard? Especially since two of our crewmen have already been captured?" Rusus asked.

"It has been months since those crewmen were captured and nothing has happened," Blassen stated confidently. "Besides, the League of Universal Planets has no gripe with us and, remember, no one will know who the girls are. That's the beauty of the whole plan."

Diane and Robin awoke early the next morning, and it would prove to be a very long day. Their talkative friend wouldn't say a word to them, except his usual, "Nourishment," and the food he brought was as bad as the day before.

Despite their fear, they were going crazy with boredom. They knew it was bad when they found themselves looking forward to dinner, still a few hours away. The horrible food would at least give them something to talk and complain about as they tried to decipher what it was.

Robin suddenly giggled and Diane stared at her. "What's so funny?"

"I am so bored. This is even worse than Ensign Bryson's lecture!"

Lieutenant Barbara Carin, the girls' teacher, was not feeling well, and Ensign Joshua Bryson had been assigned to teach their class. He was very tall, blond, and extremely nerdish. Rumor had it that he had won a dance competition when he was at the Academy, but neither Robin nor Diane could ever imagine him on the dance floor—although they always got a good laugh trying to picture it.

Bryson's topic for the day: how to coordinate and log the computer library files. As far as the girls were concerned, it couldn't get much worse than this.

The sisters sat next to each other in the back of the room where they always sat, their desks touching. The other kids were scattered around the room, also looking bored, but more or less paying attention, except for Jared. Diane was sure he was actually sleeping, his head carefully concealed in his arms. He has the right idea, *she thought.* Well, he is the smartest kid in the class.

Diane sat with her arms folded on the desk and her head resting on them, listening to Bryson's monotone voice drone on and on. She shifted impatiently in her chair, counting the minutes until recess. Much more of this and she was going to scream. But when she looked over at her sister, she had to stifle a laugh.

Robin was smiling happily, seemingly unconcerned with Bryson's lecture. She was doing a finger-dance on her desk—hands next to each other, fingers bent, tips touching the desk and moving to the music she heard in her head—a dance in honor of their new instructor. One, two, three, index fingers up and kicking. One, two, three, middle finger's turn to kick. Robin's fingers looked like a little kick line moving in precise timing. Two hands made it look good, but four hands would definitely be better, so Diane joined, adding her hands next to Robin's for a fabulous four-handed finger kick line!

The girls couldn't help but giggle while doing it. Unfortunately, the giggling turned into uncontrollable laughter, and Ensign Bryson appeared at their desks. Luckily, he hadn't seen what they were doing, but asked instead, "Would you like to share your amusement with the rest of the class?" The question brought on even more peals of laughter, and they could only shake their heads to indicate a definite 'no.'

"Then could you please stop laughing?" he asked authoritatively, but his high-pitched voice didn't match his demeanor. He didn't do 'stern' very well.

Both girls nodded their heads to imply they would, but they couldn't do it. The laughter just kept coming. By now the rest of the class was laughing too, even though nobody had any idea what the joke was. Bryson had lost control of the whole room.

"I think it would be best if you stepped outside with me," was all he could think to say. Diane and Robin followed him into the corridor, both hysterical, doubled over, stamping their feet, and barely able catch their breath.

Ensign Bryson couldn't believe his luck, and the girls couldn't believe their lack of it...just as they stepped outside the classroom, the captain and Gerroll rounded the bend.

"Is there a problem here, Ensign?" Marsh inquired, although he knew the answer just by the look on the poor man's face, and the uncontrollable laughter coming from his daughters.

"Well, Sir, the girls seem to have found something funny. They won't stop laughing, the whole class is hysterical, and I've lost control of everything," Bryson admitted and shook his head in chagrin.

"I see. Would you like me to handle this?" Marsh asked, trying to resist a smile.

"Please, Sir." Bryson's face was one of pure gratitude.

Marsh turned to his second-in-command. "Gerroll, I'll meet you back on the bridge in a few minutes. I need to handle this first," he said, shaking his head and wondering what the cause of the outburst was this *time.*

"Yes, Captain," Gerroll said, but would have preferred to stay and find out what the girls were laughing about. He hoped they would tell him later.

"You two come with me," Marsh said, and with a hand on each of their backs, he led his daughters into his office. He left them standing in front of his desk, took his seat, sat back, and waited.

Robin took a sidelong glance at Diane, a broad smile slowly sliding across her face. Diane bit the inside of her cheeks and pressed her lips together, trying desperately to suppress another burst of laughter, but as she caught Robin's look, she couldn't help it. Unfortunately, it came out as a snort, and this made the girls laugh even harder.

They tried to stop, would actually manage it for a second or two, catch their breath, look at each other, and then start again. It took a good five minutes, but they finally stopped. The silence was almost deafening.

"I would like to know what you were doing that was so funny," Marsh said, trying hard not to get sucked into their laughter. He had no doubt it was their behavior that had caused this outburst.

The girls knew there was no way he would allow them to leave without a full explanation, so Robin bravely walked up to his desk and did a finger-dance for him. Diane joined her, and he got a full demonstration of the four-handed finger kick line, just as they had done in the classroom.

Unfortunately, it started the giggles all over again, and this time Marsh couldn't help himself—their laughter was contagious. When they had all composed themselves, Marsh sent the girls back to the classroom with a promise to apologize to Ensign Bryson, and then spend the next three afternoons helping him catalog and log computer library files.

Marsh's daughters would never know that, after they left, in the privacy of his office, he tried to do a finger-dance.

"Commander," the science officer yelled to Blassen. "We are approaching the portal, but my sensors show a magnetic storm along the eastern sector."

Blassen sat rigid in his chair. "We can't delay. Plot a course through and try to avoid the storm."

"The portal isn't big enough for us to escape the storm completely," his officer said, trying to reason with his commanding officer.

Blassen's loud, booming voice echoed through the bridge, demanding obedience from all within earshot. "We go in anyway! Raise shields and prepare for a rough ride."

The science officer sighed. No one argued with Blassen.

Dinner was as bad as Diane and Robin predicted, but this time it proved to be lucky they didn't eat much. Shortly after they pushed their plates away, they felt a shift in the ship's movements. They didn't know what it was, but they suddenly felt very peculiar. Within seconds, they felt as if their bodies were compressing, and they doubled over with nausea. Then the ship started rolling and tossing. The girls tried to grab onto something, but there was nothing within reach, so they rolled and tossed along with the ship. It seemed to go on forever but, in truth, it lasted only a few minutes. The turbulence stopped as suddenly as it had started, and the ship resumed its normal pattern of flight.

"Are you okay, Robin?" Diane asked as they stood up and checked for bruises.

"I…I think so. You?"

"Yeah."

"What happened?"

The girls looked at each other blankly. It was a question neither could answer. They had no way of knowing that the portal the ship had just crossed through had taken them further away from home than they ever could have imagined.

"Commander, we are through the portal, but the ship has been damaged," the officer in the engine room reported. Blassen was relieved that they had made it through. He could deal with the damage later.

"How bad?" he asked.

"The engines are off-line. We have impulse power only. The shields are damaged. Until the engines are back to full power, we can't use the camouflage device or the probe."

"How long will it take until we can use them?"

"We won't have full power until we find a space station."

Blassen scowled at the thought of making an unscheduled stop.

"Navigator, where is the closest space station?" Blassen demanded, annoyed at the inconvenience.

"The closest station is in LUP space. To reach a Frazon space station, we will have to go days out of our way."

Things were getting worse by the second. He didn't want to waste the days needed to reach the Frazon space station. "How long until we reach the LUP station?"

"Fifteen hours at this speed. By tomorrow morning."

"Plot the course!" Blassen bellowed. Traveling through LUP space was one thing, but he didn't like the idea of stopping at an LUP space station with his two captives aboard. Not that anyone would know them since they had already crossed the portal, but still, it was risky.

Blassen turned to his trusty sycophant. "Rusus!" he called.

Rusus was at his Commander's side in seconds. "Yes, Commander?"

"See to it that your charges sleep the entire time we are at the space station."

CHAPTER 8

MILK...NO WAY!

Breakfast, if you could call it that, was late, and Diane and Robin wondered the whereabouts of their taciturn waiter.

"He probably decided not to bother coming since we don't eat anyway," Robin suggested.

"Maybe we insulted him. He could be the chef."

"Then he deserved to be insulted. His cooking is even worse than mine," Robin admitted.

Diane grinned and nodded, but didn't argue. Robin hated to cook, and her endeavors made that perfectly clear.

"Come on…my cooking's not *that* bad!" Robin paused, then asked meekly, "Is it?"

"Well, you run a close second to whoever does the cooking here."

"Well, if that's how you feel, I'm never cooking for you again. You can starve before I—"

Diane's head snapped toward the door. "Rob, he's here!"

Sure enough, the silent waiter was back with his little tray.

"No bowls this time," Diane said quietly as she glanced at the tray. "He must be getting the hint."

Instead, the trays held two large black glasses, which he put down on the table. The girls expected him to leave as he always did, but he picked up one of the glasses and handed it to Diane. She took it and exchanged looks with Robin. Seems he was going to stay and make sure they drank. Diane looked into the glass and then back at him.

"I'm not drinking this," she said and tried to hand the glass back to him. "I think it's milk," she whispered to her sister, "or something that looks just like it." Diane hated milk…wouldn't touch it.

"No way," Diane said to him, still trying to give the glass away. "I won't."

"Drink that or I will use this," he said, his hand going into the pocket of his robe. Those were the first words he'd spoken to them aside from his usual, "Nourishment." He pulled out the biggest pressure injector either girl had ever seen, probably geared for his species' large frames.

Diane's eyes grew wide and she didn't know where to look first, at the glass of milk or the injector, another item high on the list of things she hated. The thought of an injection from that thing made her shudder. She contemplated the worse of two evils and concluded she had no intention of doing either.

Diane glanced at Robin, the glass, the injector, and then back to Robin. She smiled at her sister, a smile Robin understood instantly—and she knew just what to do.

Without thinking twice, Diane splashed the entire glass of milk-stuff in his face, surprising him just long enough for Robin to grab the injector out of his hand. Before he could gain his composure, she loaded it and plunged it into his arm.

For a split second, they didn't think it was going to work. He came at them, grabbed onto Robin's arm and pulled her toward him. She struggled to get away, but he held onto her. Then suddenly, as the drug hit him, he released his grip on her, staggered, and then hit the floor faster than a ton of bricks off a short table.

"Wow, it's true," Diane said, staring at their captor sprawled on the floor.

"What?" Robin asked as she tried to catch her breath.

"'The bigger they are, the harder they fall!'" Both girls laughed, something they hadn't done in a while, and it felt very, very good.

"Let's get out of here," Robin said, pulling her sister toward the opening in the force field.

"Wait," Diane said, freeing her arm from Robin's hand. "Check his robe. See if he has anything we can use. I'll get the robes in the bathroom and we'll put them on over our clothes. If that's what they wear on this ship, we won't look as conspicuous."

"Good thinking!" Robin said, and then yelled, "Look what I found!" She held up another injector.

"That one has *your* name on it! He probably brought one for each of us in case we didn't drink the drugged milk."

They slipped on the robes and left the cell for the first time in more than three days.

The corridors were quiet. The only person the girls had seen was the alien now lying on the floor in their cell. They had no idea how many more aliens were on the ship.

The sisters walked slowly, looking stealthily around as they went but, of course, nothing was familiar. The signs on the doors were in a language they couldn't read, and they didn't dare enter any rooms.

"Shhh," Robin whispered. "Someone's coming."

They ducked into a doorway to hide. Luckily, everything was oversized, matching their abductors' proportions, and the doorway gave them both ample space to squeeze into.

One huge alien rounded the bend and quickly entered the room across from where they were standing. When the door securely closed behind him, the girls tiptoed over and pressed their ears to the door. Unable to understand the alien's strange language, the girls looked at each other and shrugged, frustrated by their inability to comprehend what was happening. But then came a sound they *did* know.

"It's the transporter room!" Diane announced gleefully as they heard the familiar sound of the transporter being activated.

"I only heard two voices," Robin said. "And one of them just transported down. That leaves only one person in there." She held up the injector and grinned. "I think we have a present for him!"

Diane nodded and smiled. "Let's go," she said, and they walked confidently through the door, catching the transporter officer off guard.

"Hi," Diane said to him. "How are you?"

He didn't react immediately, and the girls moved quickly to stand on either side of his huge body, which was draped in a blue tunic and tied at the waist with a silver cord.

"It's nap time," Diane told him in a singsong voice, as one would speak to a child.

He stared at her blankly, not understanding her language and uncertain of what to do. Taking advantage of his temporary confusion, Robin loaded the injector and drove it into his arm. He fell as quickly and loudly as his comrade. The girls smiled.

"That was almost too easy, and definitely a lot of fun," Robin said cheerfully. "Let's get out of here before our luck changes."

They stood looking at the transporter control panel. It was different from the one on the Polaris, which they were forbidden to touch, but knew how to work—at least if the coordinates were already set!

"I wonder where it's set for," Diane said.

"Who cares? It's got to be better than this place."

Diane looked at her sister and hoped that was true. "Okay, which control will activate it?" she pondered thoughtfully as she studied the board. Her hand moved tentatively around the console and then she pointed to a green touch-pad. "I say that one!"

"Try it," Robin prompted.

Diane pushed what she hoped was the correct sequence of controls, and both girls jumped onto the transporter platform. They felt the tingling of the transporter beams, and then they disappeared from the ship that had been their prison.

CHAPTER 9

Looking Back

The day-long voyage back to the Polaris seemed to go on forever. Marsh had transmitted to Gerroll the data he took from the area where the girls had been abducted. Gerroll confirmed that the same probe had been used there and to scan the Polaris. *Who would take my girls… and why?* The unanswered questions were driving Marsh crazy. He tried to clear his mind, but all he could think about was his daughters…

There had been three Marsh brothers—Daniel, Brad, and William. Despite the fact that the brothers were each three years apart, they could almost pass as triplets. Handsome and rugged, with dark wavy hair and those sparkling green eyes, they turned heads. One glance at their father, Jake, and it was clear where the boys had gotten their looks. Sarah Marsh, their fair-haired, brown-eyed mother, grouped her husband and sons together, simply calling them 'the Marsh Men.' Her Marsh men, she would add for emphasis. When the boys had grown, much to their mother's dismay, one by one, they left home to find their place among the stars.

Daniel, the oldest, had followed in his father's footsteps as an engineer, supervising the building of space stations, and he traveled wherever the next job took him.

Brad, the middle brother, was a virologist who dedicated his life to medical research. Teams of researchers were needed to combat the host of new diseases brought about by the never-ending exploration of the galaxy.

Bill, the youngest, had pursued his boyhood dream and entered the Intergalactic Academy of Space Studies. He graduated number one in his class, the first step of many that would hurl him toward his ultimate goal of starship captain.

Bill's first assignment after graduating had been on the Columbia, a minor starship. The Columbia had been sent on a diplomatic mission to Overlan, a small planet that was under intermittent attack from her neighboring planet, Romana. Overlan had the better of the two locations, perfectly located from their sun, and its natural resources were in abundance. The people were peaceful and gentle and would have been happy to share their resources with Romana. The people of Romana, though, were not so cooperative. Unlike their neighbors, their more hostile environment had made them a more hostile people, and they wanted total control of both planets. But the inhabitants of Overlan would never willingly give up their freedom. What had begun as a minor dispute between the two planets was promising to become a major interplanetary war if something wasn't done soon.

Overlan was a member of the League of Universal Planets, whose major function was to unite and protect member planets. The rulers of Overlan had called on the LUP to help solve their disputes with Romana. The LUP, in turn, had contacted Space Central, which had replied by sending the Columbia. It was a mission that might take a few months—for peace would not come easily to these two planets—but that was okay by the young Ensign William Marsh.

Marsh's brother, Daniel, and his wife, Beth, were living on Overlan. Except for a brief visit to attend their wedding, Marsh had been caught up in his studies at the Academy and hadn't had a chance to see his brother and sister-in-law in almost two years. Beth, a scientist, was doing medical research, and Daniel was between projects.

Daniel was thrilled that his little brother's mission had brought him to Overlan, if only for just a short while. It was an exciting time. He and Beth were going to be parents.

Beth was due to give birth within the month. They could have found out if the baby was male or female, but Daniel and Beth had taken the old-fashioned route and opted for a surprise. Marsh was glad that he'd get a chance to see his nephew or niece before he left.

Within a week of Bill's arrival on Overlan, Daniel was called away to check the plans for the space station he would be working on. He'd only be gone a week, but he wasn't happy about leaving so close to the baby's birth. The doctor promised him that the baby wouldn't be born for at least another two, maybe three weeks and so, reluctantly, Daniel left.

The baby, though, had other plans. Daniel had been gone only a day when Beth went into labor. Not wanting to be alone on such a monumental day, she contacted Marsh and asked if he would accompany her to the hospital. Luckily, she had caught him while he was off duty, and he was able to transport down and go with her. This was new territory for Marsh. With a career in Space Central ahead of him, he hadn't planned to marry any time soon, and babies were something he never even thought about. But this baby would make him an uncle, so he went along to give any assistance he could.

Beth's doctor, Dr. Janet Harper, was there to meet them as soon as they arrived at the hospital. Marsh was ushered to a waiting area, and Beth was immediately taken to delivery. This baby seemed to be in a hurry. Sure enough, less than an hour later, before he could even finish the article he was reading, Marsh was asked, in absence of the father, if he would like to come see his new niece.

Marsh checked on Beth, who was doing fine, and turned to see Dr. Harper holding a small bundle out to him. On April 8th in the year 2284, Bill Marsh held his first infant. Her name, Beth told him, was Diane. Marsh couldn't believe how small she was. He knew babies were little, but was shocked by just how tiny she really was—five or six pounds at the most.

"Six pounds, four ounces, and eighteen inches long, to be exact," the nurse informed him.

Marsh touched his niece's palm with his index finger, and she wrapped her tiny, perfect hand around it. An instant connection was made. He was enthralled.

"Babies do that instinctively," Dr. Harper told him, but Marsh didn't care. This child was special; she was his *niece. For the first time in his life, in a wave so strong and immediate, he understood the strength and pull of paternal love. Marsh was simply overwhelmed and felt as if he could hold this bundle forever. He sighed sadly and gave Diane back to the nurse. He was thrilled for Daniel and Beth, but a little sad for himself because he suddenly realized that the path he was taking would never allow him that kind of joy.*

The rate at which babies grew and changed amazed Marsh. He didn't see his niece every day, and it seemed that every time he did see her, she was bigger and doing something new. Daniel and Beth laughed at his constant amazement and always took advantage of his offers to baby-sit. His shipmates thought he was just plain crazy, but Marsh knew he wouldn't be on Overlan for much longer, and he was trying to cram as much as possible into a few short months. He knew that once he left he probably wouldn't see his niece again for many years. He tried not to think about it, but that was the reality of a life in Space Central.

Diane was a good baby. So good, in fact, that Daniel and Beth decided to have another. Diane and her sibling would be less than a year apart.

Marsh's time to leave came when Diane was not quite four months old. Peace had not yet been established between the two warring planets, but the Columbia had other missions, and Space Central was sending another ship to take her place.

Diane knew her uncle well by then and smiled a toothless grin at him. Marsh wondered if she'd remember him when he was gone, but knew better. She was too young to have any cognitive memory of their time together, and the next time he saw her she'd be introduced to him as if he were a total stranger.

Marsh hugged his niece and said his goodbyes to Daniel and Beth, who promised to call him as soon as the new baby was born. He left with mixed emotions, excited to be on his way to other missions, but sad for what he was leaving behind.

Marsh tried to keep in touch with Daniel and Beth, but he was so busy. Luckily, every few weeks his computer would flash a new holograph or video of his niece that his brother or Beth would send, which would prompt him to contact them.

In the beginning of December he received a hologram wishing him happy holidays, so he took a few minutes to return the greetings. As always, he played a little virtual peek-a-boo with his niece…her favorite game. Every time he moved his head from her view he would hear her giggle…his favorite sound. It was hard to believe she was almost eight months old. She was getting big—and soon she would have a sibling! The new baby would be born sometime the beginning of March.

As it turned out, the holidays would be far from happy

that year and looking back, Marsh was grateful for those moments he had taken to speak with Daniel and Beth.

The day had started with Daniel and Beth rushing around their small house trying to get their schedules straight.

"I have so much to do today!" Beth exclaimed. She was dressing herself and Diane at the same time.

"Let me help you," Daniel said and took his daughter to finish dressing her. When he was through, he held her high in the air above his head and jiggled her until she giggled at him.

Beth watched and smiled. "Better put her down, Daniel, before you wear her breakfast!"

"Good idea," he agreed quickly and cradled his daughter in his arms instead. "Better idea…have lunch with me today, Beth. Diane will be with the sitter and we can relax for a while."

Beth walked over to him, kissed her daughter and then her husband. "Only if you help me pick up some equipment I need at the medical building afterwards."

"You've got a deal," Daniel said. "Meet me at my office at noon."

Daniel surprised Beth with a picnic lunch that he had set up under a tree not far from his office. He remembered everything, including a bunch of freshly picked flowers.

"Oh, Daniel…flowers!" Beth cooed when he handed them to her. "Where did you get them?"

"Well, I…uh…picked them…from over there," he

admitted sheepishly and pointed to the landscaping outside his office.

Beth chuckled at her husband's embarrassment. "Well, I love you anyway," she assured him and threw her arms around him.

"Wait, there's more," he told her mysteriously.

"More? What? What is it?" she asked, clapping her hands excitably, like a little girl waiting for a surprise.

He reached into the bag and pulled out a yellow blanket, which he chivalrously laid down for her. She made a show of sitting down, and then pulled him down to sit with her.

After lunch, she put her head on his lap and looked up into the tree as they talked while he played with the honey-colored curls that framed her face. Every once in a while she'd interrupt him to point out a bird that would come to visit.

As with their first child, Daniel and Beth opted not to know the gender of the baby, and they spent the hour speculating what the surprise would be. They even picked a name. Well, Daniel did. He knew what name he wanted if it was a girl, but they couldn't decide on a boy's name. There was no rush; they still had three months to think about it.

"I hate to say it," Beth said sadly, "but we have to get going. I need to get that equipment for my work this afternoon."

Daniel helped his wife to a sitting position—moving was hard for her these days—then pulled her to her feet. She fell into his arms for a sweet after-lunch kiss and embrace.

They packed up the remains of their picnic and headed for their destination. They strolled slowly, holding hands and relishing each other's company, the sunshine, and the soft breeze that smelled of flowers and trees.

Halfway to the medical building, the skies suddenly blazed with Romana warships. Life had been so peaceful lately that the inhabitants of Overlan had almost forgotten about their warring neighbors. The attack was unprecedented—and unexpected. The sky crackled with phaser blasts, and the ground erupted with explosions. Smoke and debris were everywhere. The beautiful day of seconds before was gone.

"BETH!" Daniel screamed and rushed to shield his wife, but he was killed instantly by one of the first blasts. Beth was thrown a few feet from him and severely wounded by the falling wreckage of a once-stately building. The air was filled with the screams of surprised and wounded pedestrians. It had happened so quickly, no one knew what to do. The streets were instant pandemonium.

Dr. Harper came running from the medical building, medical kit in hand, and went searching for wounded civilians to help. The first person she came upon was Beth. With one instinctive look, she knew Beth wouldn't live much longer, but hoped she could save her baby. She swiftly moved her into the hospital and, in a matter of minutes, she delivered another baby girl, three months premature and weighing less than three pounds.

Beth gazed lovingly at her new daughter. She gently kissed the baby's tiny head and, with her last breath, gave her daughter the name Daniel had chosen just moments before… Robin. On December 8th in the year 2284, eight months to the day after her sister, Robin was born into a world without parents.

Daniel and Beth had had the foresight to make arrangements for their children in case something should happen to them. Their last recorded instructions left William Marsh, the girls' uncle, as their legal guardian.

Dr. Harper was surprised they would choose a man who had dedicated his life to Space Central. She had been impressed with the young man the night they met, but she had a feeling that Marsh was someone who put his military duties above all else. He was scheduled to arrive in two days, and Dr. Harper wondered what he would do with two small babies now in his permanent care.

Dead. Both of them. It must be a mistake, Marsh thought. But it wasn't a mistake. The message had been quite clear. He closed his eyes, lay down on his bed, and let the knowledge flood his mind. As a tear slid down his cheek, he realized that he had to contact his parents, a task he was not looking forward to.

Aside from the subspace messages he and his parents routinely exchanged, he hadn't spoken to them in months. Eight months to be exact. On the night Diane was born, he had contacted them with the wonderful news. Now he had the wonderful news of Robin's birth, and the tragic news of Daniel and Beth's death. His parents would be crushed.

He needed their help, though. Dr. Harper had contacted him from the hospital, where she was taking care of both babies, and informed him that he had been named the girls' legal guardian. He had sat in total disbelief, staring at the viewscreen. What was he going to do? Refusing Daniel and Beth's last request was not an option. He was honored that they had entrusted him with Diane and Robin, and he had every intention of fulfilling their final wishes. But he couldn't take two infants into space with him. When the girls were older, absolutely, but certainly not now.

For this one, Marsh needed his parents. Hopefully, they would agree to take the girls until he could make alternate arrangements. He hated to do this to them, but he could think of no other way.

He shouldn't have worried. His parents insisted that Diane and Robin come back to the Turquoise Trail Ranch with them. They assured Marsh that they would be thrilled to raise the girls until he could look after them himself. They had raised three boys—"And done a great job at it!" his mother declared—and now they would raise two granddaughters. If they couldn't have Daniel back, at least they could care for his daughters. They would catch the first transport vessel they could and meet him on Overlan.

He, too, had arrangements to make.

Captain Kylander had given him time to get the girls settled, but also told him to return to his duties as soon as he could. "There are matters here that need your attention as well," he had said.

It was as if he had two lives, and they were as different as day and night. But he knew that just as the light of dawn and the dark of night formed to make a whole and perfect day, he would find a way to join his two worlds so that he, too, could remain whole.

The flight to Overlan had been uneventful. Marsh spent the time rehashing everything that had happened, as if by some miracle an answer would suddenly and miraculously emerge. Dr. Harper met him with a hovercar and personally brought him to the hospital. Marsh couldn't believe what had happened to the lovely landscape he remembered. He sat in stunned silence, watching the remnants of the city go by as Dr. Harper brought him up-to-date on his nieces' status.

"Robin is progressing nicely and her overall health is excellent," Dr. Harper informed him with a smile. "She eats voraciously and at this rate should be at the proper weight in no time. At that point, I'll determine whether she is strong enough to make the trip back to Earth."

Marsh listened and nodded uncertainly. Dr. Harper put a hand on his arm. "She'll be fine, Bill. Really."

"And Diane? How is she?" Marsh inquired, trying not to sound as anxious as he felt.

"Understandably, she had been confused and frightened, but has adjusted nicely and is doing well," Dr. Harper reassured him as they left the hovercar and climbed the steps that led to the hospital.

Marsh knew that both girls were too young to understand the recent events and, unfortunately, neither would have any memory of their parents. It would be up to him to keep Daniel and Beth alive in their hearts. He took a deep breath before entering the hospital and steeled himself to meet his future.

The hospital was crowded with casualties from the attack, and he found Diane in the nursery, safely tucked in *the arms of a young nurse. When he approached, Diane hid her face in the nurse's shoulder; Marsh was sure she didn't recognize him. When she poked her head up, he smiled at her. She hesitantly returned his smile and continued to play peek-a-boo with him. He moved closer, and she giggled. Finally, a hint of recognition from their subspace games crossed her small face and she reached her arms out to him. He picked her up, and she snuggled into him as if it were the most natural thing for her to do. Much to his surprise, it felt just as natural to him. He sighed a deep sigh of relief, and then turned his attention to Robin.*

Despite Dr. Harper's assurances that Robin was going to be fine, Marsh was scared. How could someone so small and delicate survive? *he wondered. He remembered how he thought Diane had been so tiny when she was born, but she had been a giant next to Robin. He was sure that he could hold this baby in the palm of his hand.*

He gently stroked Robin's hand with his finger, almost afraid to touch her, in fear that she might break. But once again, he felt a tiny hand wrap around his finger—and he was caught in a storm of overwhelming emotions.

Uncle by birth, father for life.

Diane and Robin were no longer his nieces, they were his daughters, and he would do whatever he had to do to keep them safe.

Marsh watched the girls with different eyes now and realized that the eyes of a father are very different from those of an uncle. It was all so new to him, and he was suddenly worried about everything. His mother patiently explained to him what he needed to know, and he was grateful for her presence. They all remained at the hospital until Robin gained strength, and it surprised Marsh that in no time at all everything became second nature—from changing diapers to telling bedtime stories.

The days and weeks went quickly, and Dr. Harper finally announced it was safe for Robin to travel with his parents back to the ranch. It was a difficult parting. Marsh wasn't sure when he would be able to see his girls again, let alone hold them. He didn't get much shore leave, but he promised to come home as soon as possible. He had no idea, standing on the platform seeing them off, how fast time flies when one has children.

He might have been physically absent, but Marsh was able to speak with his daughters often, sometimes every night before they went to sleep if he was within communication range. He'd see them on the viewscreen and long to hold them. He looked forward to hearing those excited, magical words, "Daddy, guess what!" which were followed by an array of stories that always made him smile. He heard about their days, their accomplishments, their disappointments, and especially about their mischief. He heard a lot about that! He wondered how two little girls could possibly find so much trouble, but they always managed, even at a young age. He got home as often as he could, but it was never enough for any of them.

When they were five years old, Marsh began to think about taking the girls with him into space. The partings were becoming too difficult for all concerned. It had been a hard decision to make. Diane and Robin loved their grandparents, the ranch, and their horses. He worried they wouldn't want to leave. He also worried that being brought up on a starship wouldn't be in their best interest.

Plus, his mother didn't want them to go. She wouldn't say so, but he could tell. He had come home on shore leave with the intention of making a decision, but he was beginning to think there would be no resolution to his dilemma. An almost tragic turn of events made the decision for him...

It had been a nice, quiet afternoon. Robin was sitting in a pile of sand carefully inspecting some rocks, Diane was standing at the corral watching the horses, and Marsh and his parents were having another conversation about the girls' future. He glanced at Robin and was amazed at the intent look on her face as she turned a specimen over and over in her hand. He looked at Diane, her eyes bright with joy as she pet each horse that came to greet her at the fence.

The horses were getting restless. It would soon be time to let them out of the corral for the evening. They would go up into the meadow for the night to graze and come back in the morning for their breakfast of hay and oats.

Diane was standing on the fence and turned to ask him if she could go into the corral. "Daddy, pleeease," she begged.

"Absolutely not—it's much too dangerous," he warned. She pouted, hoping to make him change his mind, but he sternly shook his head. Finally, she nodded in understanding, and he went back to his conversation.

When Marsh looked back a few seconds later, she was gone from the fence. He looked around but didn't see her.

A glance at Robin showed she hadn't gone to sit with her sister, and he was beginning to get nervous. Then, from the corner of his eye he spotted a head of dark curls moving among the flowing manes and swishing tails of the horses. She had gone into the corral despite his warning.

As she made her way through the crowded corral, the horses became increasingly agitated, and Marsh watched as a large, chestnut stallion in the corner reared up, which started a chain reaction of panicking horses.

Marsh moved as quickly as he could. He'd seen people trampled by horses, and the thought of that happening to his child was terrifying. He jumped the fence and, in that moment, he realized something with amazing clarity—he wanted his girls with him. He wanted them where he could watch over and protect them. They would leave with him, and he would have to hope that he was making the right decision. He scooped Diane up, and her arms went around his neck searching for the safety she knew she would find. She rested her head on his shoulder, and he felt her hot, wet tears through his shirt as she held him tightly. He wasn't sure if she was afraid of the danger in the corral or because she knew she hadn't listened to him. Either way, he hated to see her cry. He carried her back to safety and into the house.

His mother watched as he hopped the fence, and she knew what he knew—they were his daughters, and he'd protect them at all costs…with his life, if need be. She sighed and looked at her husband, who nodded in confirmation. The girls belonged with their father, and she was going to lose them *to the stars as well.*

Marsh brought Diane up to her room and, while he

gently wiped the tears from her dark eyes, he quietly and calmly explained to her that there were consequences for not listening to him. When he told her she couldn't go anywhere near the horses for two days, she screamed and cried and told him over and over how much she hated him. For effect, she slammed her door whenever he left her room. Wait until she finds out there are no doors to slam on a starship, he thought with a smile.

The girls didn't need convincing to leave with him… they wanted to be with him. Yes, they would miss the ranch and their grandparents, but there was no question that they wanted to go. Even Diane had finally forgiven him and couldn't wait for the journey to begin.

They only had one question for him… "Daddy, are there horses to ride on a starship?"

It had been an adjustment for all of them, but once aboard the starship, Marsh and his girls fell into an easy routine that seemed to work for everyone. The girls enjoyed living in space and they loved being with their father.

Marsh brought them down to as many planets as he could, and he taught them about different races and cultures, expanding their horizons far beyond those of other children their age. He even found horses—or a species close enough—for them to ride.

Diane and Robin were rarely apart, always each other's best company. To Marsh, that was a blessing. A life in the military was a transient one. As he got promoted, he got transferred. He went where it was best for his career, and the girls went with him. Diane and Robin were outgo-

ing and friendly, but it was difficult to keep friends when moving around as often as they did.

Marsh was the one constant in his daughters' lives, and they in his—and they still enjoyed time with their grandparents. He had promised his parents that the girls would return to the Turquoise Trail Ranch for two months every summer.

It was during the summer of 2294, while Diane and Robin were away, that Marsh was promoted to captain of the Polaris. At age thirty-four, Marsh had become the first captain of the newly commissioned starship…the flagship of the fleet. Her massive hull, which enclosed sixty-four decks and housed two thousand, eight hundred sixty-five crewmembers plus nine hundred fifty-nine family members, gleamed with the anticipation of the journeys she would take with these brave explorers.

Now, Marsh watched from the shuttlecraft as the Polaris came into view. As always, when he saw her from afar, he was in awe.

"Please," he whispered in a solemn prayer to her, "help me find my girls."

CHAPTER 10

STARBASE SESTA VI

DIANE AND ROBIN materialized into the noise and bustle of—could it be?—an LUP Space Station.

"Oh, wow!" Diane shouted. "I can't believe it!"

Passersby, drawn in by the girls' excitement, couldn't help but grin as the sisters jumped up and down hugging each other. Some even paused to watch the merry scene before going on their way.

"Okay…okay," Robin said, trying to calm down and think straight. "What should we do first?"

"Get these robes off! I hate anything that reminds me of that place," Diane said emphatically. The girls ceremoniously threw the robes into the nearest trash receptacle, regaining their freedom as the robes disappeared.

"Now, we have to find the Communications Center. We've got to contact Daddy," Diane said.

They looked around excitably and stopped the first officer they saw. He gave them directions, and they ran as fast as they could. Finding their destination was the easy part. Next, they had to gain admittance. It was, after all, an LUP Space Station, patrolled by Space Central personnel, and they couldn't just barge in and ask to send a message.

"Maybe someone will recognize us," Robin suggested.

In their history classes at school, Diane and Robin had studied the era when athletes and actors had been the idols of their day—a concept the girls didn't fully understand. Exceptional ability was still admired and rewarded no matter what the profession, but it was the everyday heroes who had become the icons of people throughout the galaxy. Scientists who discovered the secrets of the universe, researchers who discovered cures for diseases, and explorers, like Marsh, who blazed new trails for humanity to follow became the subjects of holographs on children's walls everywhere.

Despite the fact that his adventures, diplomatic missions, and discoveries of new alien races to partner with had made him quite well known, Marsh shirked publicity of any kind. When he did agree to a rare photo or interview, he always kept his daughters out of it. For their protection, he said. And since individual privacy was highly respected by the media, his wishes were always respected. The girls' photos never appeared anywhere.

Diane shook her head. "I doubt anyone would recognize us," she said. "But everyone knows he has daughters, even if they don't know what we look like.

Problem is," she wondered aloud, "will anyone believe that's who we are? All of our identification was taken by those aliens when they took our communication badges."

"We'll just have to try and see," Robin said. "Should we tell anyone what happened to us?" she asked.

"I don't know, Rob. I think it's a really weird story. It's going to be hard enough to convince people who we are. Do you think anyone will also believe we've been abducted?"

"You're right. Probably not. Let's just keep the story to ourselves until we speak to Dad," Robin said, looking around. "So, how are we going to get into the Communications Station?" she asked, eyeing the security guard at the entrance.

"Maybe we should just go and ask," Diane suggested, knowing that simplicity was sometimes what worked best.

Robin laughed. Their luck had been good so far. "Why not?"

The guard asked them where they were going as they passed him.

"We're just going to see the Communications Officer…we know him. We'll only be a second," Diane explained nonchalantly, and he nodded indifferently. The girls walked casually with the air of two people who knew just where they were headed.

"I guess we don't look too threatening," Robin said, surprised, but glad by his lack of interest in them.

One officer operated the Communications Station.

They read his nameplate: Lieutenant Brian Johnston. He was seated at his post and had just taken an incoming transmission. "This is Starbase Sesta VI. How may I direct your call?"

"Well, now we know where we are," Robin whispered. "We can tell Dad."

"Can I help you?" Lieutenant Johnston asked suspiciously as the girls approached him.

"Yes, Sir," Diane said respectfully. "We need to send an emergency message."

"Really?" He leaned forward and inspected the girls. "To whom?" he asked with a dubious expression.

"To Captain William Marsh," Robin answered, and then quickly added, as she saw the shocked expression on his face, "We're his daughters."

They didn't know if he would grant their request or if he even believed them, but they were shocked when he started to laugh.

"That's a good one!" Johnston retorted, his hand banging the desk in time to his laughter. "Very original. I've heard a lot, but that one is new."

"No, really!" Diane pleaded desperately. "We have to speak to him!"

"I understand completely," Johnston said, nodding his head and trying to sound sympathetic while attempting to get his amusement under control.

Diane and Robin sighed in relief, assuming his concerned tone meant he believed them.

"My daughter has a crush on him too," Johnston said, grinning paternally.

"On who?" Robin asked, not following Johnston's line of thought.

"On Captain Marsh," he said and winked at them.

The sisters looked at each other, confused. "Ugh!" they said in unison as it hit them what he meant.

"Now, go on your way. I have work to do," he said, shooing them with his hands.

"You don't understand," Robin whined. "He really is…"

"Out! Right now! I don't want to have to call the guard. Come on girls, go!"

Diane pulled Robin out by her shirtsleeve while she was still trying to explain. "Forget it, Rob. He doesn't believe us and no one else will, either. I think we'd better come up with another idea."

CHAPTER 11

THE BABYSITTING CAPER

"Escaped? What do you mean they escaped?" Blassen screamed, his face only inches from Rusus's. He had visions of slow torture by Frazon General Malon, and of losing all those wonderful space credits from his buyer on Jastar. He wasn't sure which was worse.

"I'm sorry, Commander. I didn't expect an escape attempt. They'd been so docile up to now," Rusus explained meekly.

"Can you get the probe working?" Blassen demanded.

"No, Commander. Not until the engines are back online."

"How long?" Blassen asked gruffly, wringing his hands together to keep from choking the life out of Rusus.

"Nefan transported down to the Space Station to arrange docking privileges in their repair station."

"How long?" Blassen repeated, his voice seething.

"Six hours until we can begin repairs and then another..." Rusus swallowed hard, "...half day until the repairs are completed."

"Transport down, Rusus. And don't come back without them."

"Yes, Commander," Rusus said as he backed up to keep himself out of striking range.

Diane and Robin wandered the busy space station aimlessly, searching for some clue that might help them out of their dilemma. They stopped at a restaurant and looked in the window.

"I'm so hungry," Diane said, her mouth watering from the fragrant scents of the cooking cuisine. "The smell of the food is driving me crazy. Let's go in."

"What good will that do? We're not going to get anything without space credits," Robin said, sniffing deeply, trying to absorb the smell as if that alone could quiet her grumbling stomach.

Diane reluctantly turned away from the restaurant and glanced around the space station. "We've got to get off this station, Rob. It's only a matter of time before those goons come looking for us."

"I know. Let's see when the next transport vessel leaves for Earth."

"What good will that do? We're not going to get anything without any space credits," Diane said, in a high, squeaky voice that mimicked her sister's words. She got a slug in the arm in response.

"Yeah, well, let's find out anyway. Maybe we can think of something later."

Without difficulty, they found the transport station and the reservations desk. The clerk informed them that the next vessel left for Earth, North America, New York, at 1300 hours, less than one hour from then, at a price they couldn't afford. Then again, unless it was free, they couldn't afford anything.

Feeling dejected, discouraged, and hungry, Diane and Robin found a bench, sat down, and silently watched as people passed.

"Boy, those kids sure are noisy," Robin said, referring to the family that had taken a seat not far from them. Actually, the parents had sat down, looking tired and worn out, while their three kids ran around like wild banshees, screaming over and over that they didn't want to go to Earth.

Diane got up and pulled Robin with her. "Come with me. I have an idea. Oh, and act responsible."

Robin looked at her sister suspiciously. "Huh?"

"Come on. You'll see."

Diane approached the parents sitting on the bench. "Excuse me," she said, very politely. The harried parents turned from watching their noisy children and looked at her with a blank expression.

"My name is Diane and this is my sister, Robin. We have passes on the next transport vessel to Earth," she lied. "We're going to visit our grandparents in New Mexico. Problem is, the flight was more expensive than we thought it would be, and we only had enough credits for the fare with nothing left over for meal tickets."

Robin looked askance at her sister. *What is she up to now?* she wondered.

The couple was only partially listening, their attention focused primarily on their screaming kids who were now throwing punches at each other.

"Robin and I have spent our last few summers as…um…mother's helpers, helping this woman care for her…um…six children. We loved it. Didn't we, Rob?" Diane asked and poked her sister in the ribs to quicken her reply.

"Oh, yeah, loved it," Robin said with as much enthusiasm as she could muster, which wasn't much, considering she and Diane had never babysat for anyone in their lives.

It always amazed Robin how her sister could tell the most incredible tales with a perfectly straight face. When they pulled pranks, they thought of the ideas together, but Diane had to do the talking. When Robin tried, she always ended up laughing and ruining the whole charade, or she couldn't think fast enough and the story came out all jumbled. Not Diane—she could pull it off like a pro. But they would both have to endure the inevitable lecture and consequence from their father. He didn't care whose idea something was or who did the actual talking…if they were both involved, they were both equally culpable.

"So," Diane continued, "we were thinking that in exchange for meal tickets during the flight, we would watch your children the entire time and give you two a break. Sort of a mini vacation for you. You'd be there to supervise us, but we would keep the children occupied. We know lots of games and activities to keep them busy and we are very responsible."

The mother's head popped up to face Diane, and for the first time, the parents looked at the sisters seriously. "Give us a second to talk it over," the mother said to the girls, and pulled her husband in for a huddle.

The girls watched as the mother's long blonde hair mingled in contrast with her husband's dark hair, their heads moving together in discussion. The decision took less than a minute. "That would be great," the mother said with a sigh and weary smile, her pretty, blue eyes shining as she thought of the few quiet days she could spend with her husband.

"You've got a job!" said the father with a satisfied grin. His dark eyes looked past the girls to his screaming children. "Good luck!"

Introductions were made quickly. The parents were Ben and Cathy Farber. The children were Tim, age three; Jenny, age five; and Susie, age eight.

When the sisters had a spare second, Robin yanked Diane aside. "Okay, we can eat. How are we going to get on? We *don't* have passes, or have you forgotten that small fact?"

Pulling Robin in close so no one else could hear, Diane whispered in a conspiratorial tone, "This is my plan…keep the kids riled up and noisy. When it comes time to board, stay close by them and chase them onto the ship, right past the electronic beam. The attendant will assume the Farbers have all the passes. No one likes to deal with unruly children and, hopefully, they won't try to stop us. Once we're on, we're on—they don't check passes again—they assume you belong there. Wait until the last second and then find an empty seat."

"And assuming we can get on, what if there are no empty seats?"

"We'll duck into one of the cabins or bathrooms."

"Where will we sleep? We don't have quarters."

"When everyone is asleep, we'll sneak in and sleep on the floor in the children's quarters."

A slow smiled crossed Robin's face. "You did good! I have a feeling this might even work! But I have one more question."

Diane rolled her eyes. "What?"

"Do you think the youngest one is potty trained? I'm not changing diapers! This was your idea, so you have to change them!"

Diane opened her mouth to reply and then closed it as she thought it over. "Yeah, okay." As always, Robin thought of everything.

The plan did work. Just as they had hoped. Diane and Robin had the children so wound up and obnoxious that no one tried to stop them as they chased the kids onto the ship. Ben and Cathy Farber went through the gate, waving the electronic tickets past the beam, and no one seemed to notice that the babysitters were unaccounted for.

Their luck had continued. The ship was crowded but not full, and the girls had no problem finding two empty seats just before departure. It was a medium-sized transport vessel, which held seventy-five passengers. Diane and Robin had been on ones just like it numerous times, usually on their way to Earth for summer vacation. How different those trips were, but the sisters were never more anxious to reach their destination as they were this time.

A survey of the ship's onboard recreational facilities found them to be adequate, not nearly as good as the ones on the Polaris, but good enough to keep the children occupied and out of their parents' hair for a couple of days.

And thankfully, Tim *was* potty trained!

Dinnertime was still hours away, and the girls counted the minutes until they could eat. It seemed like ages since they had a decent meal, and once they finally sat down at the table, they had to control themselves from asking for one of everything on the menu.

Ben and Cathy ate at a different table, but kept a watchful eye over all proceedings. They were enjoying the reprieve from their children, who had taken an immediate liking to Diane and Robin, but they also sensed the girls weren't being completely truthful about their journey. Any questions were met with vague and inconclusive answers. It was evident that the girls were hiding something, but the Farbers concluded that they were probably running away from home. Ben and Cathy liked the sisters, and whatever was really going on, the Farbers hoped they could help. Diane and Robin were watching their children, but Cathy and Ben were making sure the sisters were safe too.

It had been a long day for everyone. By the time dinner was over, the children were tired, and they went to sleep easily. Although babysitting was new to the sisters, bedtime rituals were not.

"I miss Daddy," Diane said longingly. "Remember when he used to read to us?" She couldn't help but think of the bedtime rituals that she and Robin had had when they were small. Suddenly, it all seemed so long ago and far away...

Sitting in the chair opposite her father's desk, Diane waited for him to come into his office. Nervous and a little scared, she bit her bottom lip and fidgeted. She knew why she was there. She had hoped her father wouldn't find out what she had done, but when Lieutenant Diska contacted her, she knew it was too late.

"Your father said to tell you to go to his office and wait for him. He'll be there shortly," Lieutenant Diska had told her.

The worried twelve-year-old had acknowledged the order, "Okay, Lieutenant. I'm on my way." Then Helen Diska delivered the bad news, as if the fact he wanted to see her wasn't bad enough. "Diane, he knows... and he's not happy with you. I doubt he's in a good mood."

"Oh," was all Diane had managed to say. She might

have led to his bad mood, but she was hoping she could make him understand.

Marsh came in a few seconds later. Diane sat up straight in her chair and faced him as he sat down in his.

"Dad, I just wanted to—" she started to say, but he cut her off.

"It doesn't matter what you wanted, young lady. I had already told you that you couldn't."

Diane knew it wasn't a good sign when he called her "young lady." It was a term he only used when he was angry. "I know, but..."

"There are no 'buts,' Diane."

"There are, Dad, if you'll just listen to me."

"I listened this morning when you asked my permission, and I gave you my decision. I said 'No,' and I said it very clearly. You chose not to heed what I said."

"But Dad..."

"I said there were no 'buts.' Now there are only consequences." Marsh watched his daughter's face. Her eyes grew wide as if surprised by the idea he would punish her. He thought she was going to say something, but then she seemed to change her mind.

Defeat couldn't be an option. She looked past him and stared into space, trying to decide what she could say to change his mind.

"Look at me," he said sternly, and waited until her gaze returned to his face. "You're confined to your quarters for the rest of the day...and that includes tonight."

Her reaction was immediate and explosive. "NO!" she screamed. "No, Daddy, please! Not tonight!" Tonight was going to be one of the biggest parties the kids on the ship had had in months. She and Robin were heads of the planning committee and had worked for weeks to get everything perfect. They had even convinced their father to allow them to use the main lounge all evening, switching the rules from no children after 1900 hours to no adults after that time. It was going to be a great party.

Compromise, *she thought.* I'll compromise with him. *She took a deep breath and tried to remain calm. She knew from experience that if she exploded, he'd never listen.* Okay, you can do this, *she silently coached herself.* Then to her father she said, "Dad, hear me out before you say anything, please."

"Diane..."

"Please, Daddy, just listen to me. Please." *He didn't say anything, so she began her negotiations. She had to make him see, she just had to.* "Okay. You're right. I didn't listen to you, and I will take the consequences. I will. I really will. But can't we compromise?" *She thought as quickly as she could, trying to come up with the perfect solution.* "I'll stay in my quarters all day today and then go to the party tonight. In exchange for going to the party, I'll stay in my quarters all day tomorrow, and *the day after* and *I'll do whatever chores you tell me to. That's fair."

He shook his head. "I'm sorry, Diane, but I don't negotiate punishment with you. It's not for your convenience. If you wanted to go to the party, you should have thought about that before you disobeyed me."

She couldn't believe it. The compromise sounded so reasonable to her. Why wouldn't he accept it? "Dad—"

"No! There will be no more discussion. Go to your quarters…and stay there."

Jumping up from her chair, she screamed, "I HATE YOU! I DO! I HATE YOU!"

Her words stung, even though he knew she didn't really mean them. "Yes, I'm sure you hate what I've done," he said, hoping she would catch the subtle difference between hating him and hating his actions. But by the look on her face, she wasn't buying it.

She tried one last time. "Daddy, please…?" He didn't even answer; he just shook his head. She stormed out of his office, leaving him alone to contemplate the hardships of fatherhood.

Diane fell onto her bed in a torrent of tears. Robin came running from her room in the suite they shared and into her sister's room. "I guess he found out," Robin said sympathetically, but without surprise. She had tried her best to talk her sister out of doing what she had done.

"I can't go tonight," Diane cried into her pillow. "He wouldn't listen to anything I said. I tried to compromise with him and he wouldn't even listen. I hate him!"

Robin could barely understand a word Diane was saying. But even if she could, she wouldn't know how to respond, "I told you so" not being the wisest choice at this particular moment. "I'll stay with you tonight," she told her sister, instead, and rubbed Diane's back, trying to comfort her as best she could.

"No, you go. No sense in both of us missing the party.

But thanks, anyway, Rob. You're the best," Diane told her sister, then hiccupped.

Not wanting to talk to anyone, not even Robin, Diane stayed in her room all day. Robin understood. The girls were as close as two people could be, but they still needed their space. Today was Diane's day to be alone, and Robin respected that. The only time she went into her sister's room was when she was ready to leave for the party.

"Oh, Robin, you look so pretty! That dress is perfect for you!" Diane said, circling her sister to check out her new dress. Diane tried not to think about her own new outfit, which was still hanging in the closet. Robin's dress was a soft blue, lace-lined, old-fashioned peasant dress that went to her ankles. Her hair was swept up, and small curls fell gently around her face. "You look like a princess, Rob," Diane exclaimed, and Robin curtsied in response to the compliment.

"Thanks, but are you sure you don't want me to stay with you?"

"No. Go and have a good time. You'll tell me all about it when you get back."

"Okay. But I feel horrible leaving you here," Robin admitted apologetically.

"Just go, Rob," Diane said abruptly, feeling miserable, jealous, and wanting to be alone again.

Robin left reluctantly, wishing that Diane were leaving with her, but knowing there was nothing she could do to help her sister's situation.

When Robin had gone, Diane paced her quarters and reviewed her options for the evening. She could finish a *school report she was working on, read a book, play a computer game, go to sleep or…go to the party. Did she dare? She was already in trouble. Realistically speaking, what more could her father do to her?*

The new outfit beckoned. She went to her closet and pulled it out—a red jumpsuit with gold epaulets on the shoulders and shiny gold buttons that were faceted like diamonds and sparkled when they caught the light. She stared at the jumpsuit for a long time and then made up her mind. She was going to the party.

Not wanting to give herself time to reconsider the decision, she showered and dressed quickly. A fast glance at the clock told her she'd only be an hour late. She headed for the door, but stopped before it opened automatically.

This was a dangerous course she was headed on. She and Robin didn't always listen to their father, but they had never, ever disobeyed a punishment. He had taught them since they were old enough to understand that life was full of choices and there would always be decisions to make. They were free to make their own decisions, but they had to accept the consequences, whether good or bad. He gave his praise and approval easily, freely, and often for jobs well done and good decisions. Just as easily, he meted out consequences for disobedience, as he had done that morning. His response to their behavior was always immediate, and the girls invariably knew where they stood with him. There was no doubt in her mind that if she went to the party, he'd be furious with her. She shrugged it off. So what? she thought. After all, she was furious with him for not accepting her extremely reasonable compromise.

The door silently slid open as she approached it, and she stepped into the noisy corridor, but then thought twice. Quickly, she turned and stepped back into her quarters. The door closed. Maybe she should think about this for a second or two. She thought and then decided that her father was too strict and too stubborn. She stepped toward the door again. It opened again. All she had to do was walk through the opening and go to the party. Still, she hesitated. "He'll be so disappointed in me," the little voice inside her head said. She stepped back, and the door closed.

It was no use. She couldn't go. She undressed slowly, put her new red jumpsuit back on the hanger, and carefully tucked it away in the closet. Her attire for the evening was, instead, a purple and green striped nightshirt with a cluster of red velvet hearts on the right shoulder.

Sad, angry, and disappointed—at herself, at her father, and at the universe in general, she crawled into bed. The book her grandmother had given her, an old, worn copy of "Little Women" was sitting on her nightstand. Her grandmother preferred real books to computers and bought a book whenever she could locate one that was still in legible condition. She had passed on that fondness to her sons and granddaughters, and both Diane and Robin could always be found with a book close at hand.

Diane reached for the antique novel, opened to a fragile, yellowing page, and started to read. She read a few pages, but couldn't concentrate. Her brain wouldn't focus on the words, flitting instead to the random thoughts that passed, one by one, through her mind.

One of those thoughts was about the bedtime rituals

she and Robin had when they were small. The two of them would scramble into one bed and wait for their father to appear with a book. He would read to them, his deep, rich voice playing all the different characters, and they would giggle each time he changed roles. He would read until they fell asleep, then gently carry whichever daughter needed to be in her own bed, back into her room, and tuck her in for the night.

As with most childhood rituals, the bedtime stories gradually stopped as the girls grew older, leaving only a warm memory of its existence and the inability to determine exactly when it ceased to be part of the girls' evening routine. Only random thoughts, like the ones Diane had tonight, brought the memory alive again.

There was one childhood ritual that still remained, and Diane wondered if that one, like all the others, would become a thing of the past. Every night, before their father's last shift on the bridge, he stopped in to say good night. Sometimes it was just a quick visit, but most times he would stay and chat, wanting to hear about their day. Diane and Robin liked these visits. No matter how busy he was, the girls knew this was the time they had his ear, and they often saved their most important talks for his nighttime visit.

Diane picked up the book and tried to read again. She heard the outside door of their quarters open and thought Robin was back from the party. But the footsteps told her otherwise—it was her father. She dropped the book, rolled over on her side to face the wall, and pulled the covers up to her chin…she wasn't in a talkative mood this time.

Marsh knocked on his daughter's bedroom door, but got no response. He held his hand to the scanner that allowed the door to slide open, then quietly walked into her room. She appeared to be sleeping, but the room was still lit. He assumed she was playing possum, pretending to be asleep, and sat down on the side of her bed. He sat quietly for a few seconds and then decided to risk conversation.

"The day didn't turn out the way you had planned, did it?" he asked very softly.

She didn't answer but slowly shook her head.

At least she's willing to communicate, he thought. "Would you like to talk about it?" he inquired, and tenderly put his hand on her arm. With one violent movement, she jerked his hand off, and he understood her ground rules… he could talk if he wanted to, and she would tolerate his presence, but she wouldn't be an active participant in any conversation.

"I won't stay long," Marsh told his daughter. "I just wanted to tell you something. I wasn't pleased with what you did this morning, and I know you weren't happy with the consequences. Given the same circumstances, I would do the same thing again, and you need to know that. But what I came to tell you is that right now I am very proud of you." He paused and waited for a response. She didn't move. "Would you like to know why?" It took a minute, but her curiosity got the better of her and she nodded, so he continued his explanation. "I know how badly you wanted to go to the party. I was on the bridge all evening. You could have snuck out and gone anyway. But you didn't, and I'm proud of you. I wanted you to know that."

Diane wondered how he knew she hadn't gone, but chalked it up to the fact he seemed to know everything that happened, or didn't happen, on his ship.

He had only one thing more to say before he left her. "I know that you hate me, but—"

The sentence was never finished. She rolled over, sat up, and threw her arms around his neck so quickly he hardly saw it happen. "I don't hate you, Daddy. I love you! I'm so sorry," she sobbed. He held her tightly while she cried. "I love you too," he whispered. Her fingers found a soft fold of fabric on the back of his shirt and in a motion that was both calming and soothing, she caressed the satiny material between her fingers until her tears subsided.

Finally, exhausted from the emotions of day, she released the hold she had on her father's neck. She crawled back under the covers, rolled over on her side, and ended up in the same position she had started, only this time she was smiling. Marsh fixed the blanket for her, and as he did, the book she had been reading fell to the floor. He picked it up and went to put it on her nightstand, but stopped halfway there, book in hand, and sat back down on the edge of her bed.

He opened it to the bookmarked page and read to her until she fell asleep.

Diane and Robin found a quiet place on the ship to sit, and waited until they thought it would be safe for them to sneak back into the children's quarters to sleep on the floor. They sat and watched the stars go by, looking out into the darkness. Many people thought that being in space was lonely, but their father had taught them that each star and planet had its own story, and that space was rich with the history of countless civilizations. They had never felt lonely watching the stars, until now.

"I wonder what Dad is doing," Robin pondered wistfully.

"Probably wondering what we're doing."

How right she was.

CHAPTER 12

Unspoken Possibilities

He would find his children. He didn't know how. Not yet. But there was no room in his mind to even allow the possibility of defeat. His daughters were out there. He knew it. He would bring them home safely. He knew that too.

Marsh walked the Polaris expecting to see them at every turn. It was unbelievable to him that they weren't there, that he had let danger enter their lives. He second-guessed every decision he had ever made, all the way back to the one that had taken them from the safety of his parents' ranch.

Upon returning to the Polaris, his first stop had been their quarters. He sat there for what seemed an eternity, listening to the loud silence, hearing their voices and their laughter. He had never known the true meaning of torture until he sat in that empty room.

No, defeat was not a possibility. Not as long as he lived. And Marsh had no intention of doing anything to the contrary. He endured the looks of his crew and their unspoken questions for which he had no answers. Yet.

"Captain to the bridge." It was Lieutenant Diska, and her voice took him away from his thoughts.

He tapped his communication badge. "Marsh here."

"Incoming transmission, Sir. From New Mexico."

No, not now. Marsh knew he should have contacted his parents, even if just to tell them he had no news. But he hated to see the look on his mother's face, so he kept putting it off.

"Transfer the call to my quarters. I'm on my way there now." He made it just in time to see both his parents looking at him on his viewscreen, hope etched on their faces.

"I'm sorry. I don't have any news. Not yet."

"We didn't think you did, Bill," his father said, doing a good job of covering his disappointment. "You would have contacted us."

"We just wanted you to know that we're here and understand what you're going through," his mother added with a forced smile and artificial hope. "You'll find them."

Her smile, especially when he knew she didn't feel like smiling, always meant so much to him.

Marsh didn't know what to say, so he nodded his head in recognition of their encouragement. "I'll contact you as soon as I know something. Which hopefully will be soon."

It was a difficult conversation for all of them. The unspoken possibilities were endless.

"Okay, Bill, we'll wait to hear from you. We won't bother you."

"It's no bother, Dad. You know that. Contact me whenever you need to."

He ended the conversation and tried to imagine what they were feeling. Space exploration had done wonders for humanity as a whole, but had wreaked havoc on the nuclear family. It was sometimes impossible for families to stay in touch, let alone be together. Parents lost their children to outer space when they left home to settle on planets light years away. If they saw each other once a decade, it was a lot, and grandchildren were often no more than holographs and faces on viewscreens.

It had been hard for his parents when all three brothers left home and found lives in the far reaches of the galaxy. His brother Brad kept in touch, but rarely made it home. The girls hardly ever saw him, except by viewscreen every few months.

As a starship captain, Marsh's schedule left very little room for visits. He tried to schedule the Polaris's refits with the girls' yearly visits to the ranch so he could also take some shore leave, but it didn't always work out. He was glad the girls got home every summer. When Daniel was killed, his parents had been devastated, and Diane and Robin were their link to him.

Marsh knew his mother cried over the fact that she didn't see her family, and he would do everything in his power to make sure she didn't shed any more tears.

CHAPTER 13

A Very Tall Tale

"We checked the entire space station, Commander," Rusus reported. "The girls are nowhere to be found." He hated being the bearer of bad news. The commander could get very testy.

"They didn't just disappear into thin air," Blassen snorted. "They have to be there. You found no trace of them at all? I find that hard to believe, Rusus."

"We found their robes in a waste receptacle, and the girls were seen by the communications officer when they tried to reach their father," Rusus answered, relaying the information he had learned while down on the space station. "The officer was still laughing at their 'joke.' He found it very amusing when they tried to convince him Captain Marsh was their father. You were right, Commander, no one knows them."

"Of course no one knows them, Rusus, because we've gone through the portal. Did anyone else see them?"

"The reservation clerk at the transport site remembered them. They asked about the next flight to Earth, but had no space credits to pay. The clerk said they walked away very disappointed."

"Then they are still on the station," Blassen said hotly. "Hiding, but still there. I need that probe operational. I want them found."

"A few more hours, Commander. Then we'll find them."

"A lot can happen in a few hours, Rusus. Post someone down there and continue the search."

"Yes, Commander."

"And Rusus, you better start praying we find them."

Rusus sighed heavily. "Yes, Commander."

After breakfast, Ben Farber took his children off the girls' hands for a while. Diane and Robin took their break on the Observation Deck to watch the stars. It was the one place that made them feel at home. Cathy came and sat down with them, hoping to get some more information. The girls liked Cathy a lot, they really did. She seemed so concerned about them, but they couldn't take the chance of telling her anything. No one believed their story, and they didn't want Cathy to think they were crazy. So, they avoided answering the questions they could, gave nebulous answers to others, and made up stories for the rest.

Robin tried to turn the tables around and ask Cathy questions instead. "Why are you going back to Earth?"

"My husband is starting a new job in Houston."

"That's exciting," Diane said.

"Yes, it is, but the children are not happy about it. Especially Susie. She just turned eight and had a lot of friends where we were."

Diane and Robin couldn't help but notice how troubled Cathy seemed thinking about her daughter's unhappiness.

"Well, last night we told them some stories about our home on Earth, and they seemed a little better with the idea," Robin said, hoping it might ease Cathy's concern.

"Thank you very much," Cathy said, genuinely glad for their help. "It didn't seem to matter when *I* talked to them about Earth, but coming from you two makes a difference. They really look up to you girls!" She tried once more to engage the sisters in a conversation about their situation. "Do you miss your home?"

The girls nodded but didn't elaborate.

Cathy smiled at them, but was frustrated by her inability to help. Obviously, the topic wasn't open for discussion and pushing for information wouldn't help, so she chatted casually with them instead. Ben brought the children back later in the morning, and then he and Cathy went off by themselves, thankful for their babysitters.

The girls decided to make it their mission to convince Susie how great Earth was, and how much fun she'd have living there. It was the least they could do for the Farbers, who were being so good to them. They wished they could do more.

To entertain the kids, Diane and Robin took full advantage of all the ship's recreational facilities, as well as their imaginations. The children had great fun and, much to their surprise, so did the girls. Susie became their constant companion and by dinnertime, all she could talk about was going to Earth. It seemed as if they had accomplished their mission.

Ben and Cathy were amazed. Robin and Diane had done in one day what Susie's parents hadn't been able to do in three months. They all had dinner together like one big, happy family. Although they weren't home with their grandparents and father, the sisters felt as if they belonged somewhere, at least for tonight.

With dinner over, Cathy and Ben spent the evening alone while Diane and Robin put the children to bed, filling their heads with more great tales of Earth. When the children fell asleep, the girls settled in on the hard floor for the night. But it didn't matter. Tomorrow night they would sleep in their own beds. The ship was due to arrive in New York the next afternoon, and then it would be just a few hours until they were home with their father and grandparents.

Late the next morning, the captain announced that due to a meteor storm there would be a course change. Arrival time was pushed back until 0200 hours. The girls knew they would have had no trouble finding a way to contact their father and grandparents when they arrived in New York during the day, but in the middle of the night it might be harder.

"We can always ask Cathy and Ben to help us," Robin suggested. She waited for Diane to respond, but her sister was lost in thought. "Are you listening to me?"

"Robin, do you know the coordinates for the ranch?"

"Of course. Don't you?"

"Yes. I've heard Dad say them a million times."

Robin understood her sister's question. "The transporter?"

"Why not?" Diane asked. "All transport vessels have one for emergency use. It would get us home faster than first going to New York and then having to contact Dad to come get us. I just can't wait that long!"

"That's brilliant, Diane! The captain announces when we achieve orbit, and then we have a few minutes to transport down."

Diane and Robin amused the children the rest of the day while hoping their transport plan would work. They were so nervous they hardly ate lunch and skipped dinner completely. Cathy asked if they were feeling ill and didn't look as if she believed them when they said they were fine, just not hungry.

Per the Farber's instructions, the girls put the children to bed at the regular time, even though they would have to be awakened in the middle of the night for departure. The girls stayed in the children's quarters, but didn't go to sleep. They waited anxiously for the captain's announcement that the vessel had achieved orbit.

"Commander, the probe is operational," Rusus informed him.

"It's about time. Set it. Find them. NOW."

"Yes, Commander."

They all waited while the probe scanned the space station.

"Nothing, Commander. They're not there."

"IMPOSSIBLE!" Blassen bellowed and then smacked Rusus on the side of his head. "Scan again. This time at a higher intensity."

"We can't, Commander. If we do, we will burn out the space station's controls and they will start an investigation. The probe, at high intensity, is too strong for LUP technology."

"Try again at a lower intensity."

"Then we may not find them at all."

"Stop arguing with me. Just do it."

Rusus sighed and set the probe, knowing it would be useless and that he would be blamed. "Nothing, Commander. They're not there."

The next blow knocked Rusus off the chair. Blassen took the seat himself and set the probe again. Still nothing. *How can this be?* he wondered. *Where did they go?* He sat back and thought. *Where would they go? Logically, they would try to go home,* he reasoned to himself. *They must have somehow caught the transport vessel*, he realized, making the obvious, logical conclusion.

He glanced at Rusus, still sitting on the floor. "How long until all repairs are complete?"

Rusus stayed seated, expecting that his answer

would only send him back to the floor. "We have run into a few small problems, Commander."

"Problems? What kind of problems, Rusus?"

Rusus sighed. *Better get it over with,* he thought. "The main engines can't be fixed for a while."

"How long is a while?" Blassen's face was turning beet-red—not a good match with his gold eyes.

"One week, Commander." Rusus hurried the rest of the explanation, hoping to calm Blassen down. "The configuration of our engines is different from any in the LUP. They don't have the parts we need, and we will have to rebuild the engines ourselves." Rusus was shocked—and relieved—when Blassen turned and walked off the bridge without so much as a word or another blow.

The announcement finally came. Diane and Robin said silent goodbyes to the children, gathered the few items they had, and tiptoed out of the room.

"I wish we could say goodbye to Cathy and Ben," Robin said as she and Diane headed for the transporter room. "They were so nice to us."

"I know," Diane agreed. "But I have a feeling they would understand."

The girls found the transporter room easily, and it was empty as they expected it to be. They checked the control panel, but disappointment set in as they realized they didn't know what to do. The configuration of the controls was completely different from those on the Polaris.

The door to the room slid open. They were caught. But they were surprised by who it was.

"Ben!" the girls said in unison.

"I've been looking all over for you!"

"You were?" Robin asked, shocked.

"Yes. Cathy and I knew the story you told us wasn't true. When I stopped to check on the children every night, I found you asleep on their floor. We knew you snuck aboard, we just didn't know why. Cathy told me she didn't think you had any place to stay in New York, and when you weren't in the children's quarters just now, I searched the entire ship to find you. This was the last place I looked." He paused for a second then asked, "Are you running away from home? We really hoped you would tell us so we could help. We don't want you be alone. Maybe we can help patch whatever problem you are having with your family." Then he gave them a stern look edged with concern. "Besides, you're not old enough to be on your own. Your family must be worried sick about you, no matter what had happened."

"No," Diane answered. "We didn't run away. But we are trying to get back home. Honest." She pointed to the transporter panel and frowned.

"We don't know how to set the coordinates," Robin said and then blurted out without thinking, "This transporter is different than the one on the Polaris." Oops. She couldn't believe she said that. They had worked so hard at keeping their secret. Maybe he wouldn't catch it.

Diane looked over at her, stunned.

"The Polaris?" Ben asked, shocked.

Okay. He caught it. Act casual, Robin thought. "Yes, you've heard of the Polaris?" she asked, trying her best to sound nonchalant.

Diane rolled her eyes and shook her head. *Everybody* knew the Polaris…it was the most famous starship in the galaxy.

"I'm in Space Central…*Lieutenant* Ben Farber. In fact, I requested an assignment on the Polaris and I'm taking a job at Space Central headquarters until something comes through. But the Polaris has the longest list of assignment requests of all the ships in the fleet. It might be a long wait," he said. Then, looking at the girls suspiciously, he asked, "But how would you know about the transporter controls on the Polaris?"

"We know someone on her…and we…um…visit…occasionally," Robin said. She knew it was a silly thing to say, but she couldn't think of anything else.

He shook his head in frustration. "Come on, girls. If you want my help, you have to tell me the truth. What's going on?"

Robin looked at her sister. If there were ever a time for a tall tale, this was it.

Diane wanted to tell him the truth, but if he didn't believe the story, he wouldn't help, and she just couldn't take that chance. Thinking fast, she decided to give him a story with as much truth to it as she could. "Do you know Dr. Matthew Wells?"

"Yes. He's well-known around Space Central. Great doctor, I hear."

"Well, we live with our grandparents on their ranch,

which is next to Dr. Wells's parents' ranch, and his son Jared spends summers there." *That's true,* she thought.

"Okay, go on."

"The Polaris is usually in space dock getting refitted at that time, and Jared transports up to see his parents. His mother is the chief engineer." *All true.*

"Yes, I know about Lieutenant Wells."

"A couple of times, we were allowed to transport up with him. Most of the crew was on shore leave, so it was quiet." *That's stretching it…Dad would never allow friends aboard while the ship was in space dock…but kind of plausible.*

"Have you ever met Captain Marsh?" Ben asked as an aside. "I'm looking forward to serving with him."

"A couple of times, in passing. We didn't talk to him or anything." Diane said offhandedly, trying not to show her excitement that, hopefully, he would be tucking them in shortly.

Ben listened with a skeptical look. "Assuming that is all true, how would you know how to work the transporter?"

"We don't," Diane explained, "but Jared does. Please don't tell his parents…they don't know. We've watched him. It looked easy, and we thought we could do it too. But we can't. These controls look totally different." *Definitely true.*

"None of that explains what you were doing on Starbase Sesta VI."

"We had a huge fight with our father the other day and, yes, we did run away. We took our combined space credits and boarded the first transport vessel we could get, but when we got to the space station, we realized our father was right, we missed him, and we were scared, but we didn't have any credits left. Now we just want to go home." *Definitely one big, tall tale, except for the part of wanting to go home.*

"Where is your father?"

"On the ranch. He's a horse trainer." She continued to look directly at Ben and had to stifle a laugh when she heard Robin's subtle gasp.

"Okay, you're almost out of time," Ben said, deciding to believe them. "Give me those coordinates." He fed them into the transporter while Diane and Robin jumped onto the platform.

"Please say goodbye to the children," Robin said.

"And Cathy," Diane added.

Together they called, "Thank you, Ben!" just as they felt the tingle of the transporter that was going to send them home.

Diane and Robin materialized on the field behind the barn.

"A horse trainer? Really?" Robin said, giggling.

"He'll think it's funny. I can't wait to tell him! Let's go!"

The lights in the house were out, and the night was black and silent. The girls shivered from the sudden coolness of the late night desert air. The sisters looked up into the clear night sky, amazed that's where they had just come from.

They couldn't believe they were home! All they

wanted was their father. They ran at top speed up the porch steps and had to stop short from crashing into the front door. Robin put her hand up to the computerized lock so it could read her pre-programmed handprint and waited to hear the opening click. Nothing.

Diane tried. The lock didn't unlatch. "It must be broken," she said.

They started banging on the door.

CHAPTER 14

THE TWILIGHT ZONE

"Who could it be at this time of night?" Sarah Marsh asked her husband. She swung her feet out of the old-fashioned four-poster bed they shared and grabbed for her robe while her feet tried to find her slippers.

"I don't know," Jake Marsh said, still half asleep. "But by the banging on the door, we're going to find out soon enough." He pushed aside the lace curtains as he slipped on his robe and looked out the window that overlooked the front porch. "It's two young girls. I don't recognize them from here. Maybe they're a couple of the neighbor's kids or grandkids."

The loud, desperate banging continued, made even louder by the stillness of the night.

"Okay, okay. Hold on. We're coming!" Jake yelled. They both ran down the stairs in a race to get to the door and stop the noise before the whole ranch was awakened, the lights in the house turning on as they passed the motion detectors.

No sooner had the latch scanned his hand and unlocked the door, when these two young strangers were inside hugging them, while crying and talking at the same time. Through the tears and hysteria, the girls talked excitably about having been so scared and afraid they'd never get home. They kept asking repeatedly, through every disjointed sentence, "Where's Daddy?" and finally demanding, "Get Daddy. Please get Daddy!"

It was hard enough to be woken up in the middle of the night, but then to be thrown into this kind of confusion was disarming. Even more confusing was that these girls kept calling them "Grandma" and "Grandpa" and referring to "Daddy" as if they were supposed to know who that was. The elder Marshes looked at each other, utterly puzzled and flabbergasted.

Jake tried his best to take control. He led the girls into the living room to sit on the couch, but they wouldn't sit down. "Calm down. Relax. Stop crying," he said over and over. Easier said than done. The harder he tried to quiet them, the louder they became.

Not knowing what to do, but recognizing the fact they were just children and certainly panicked, Jake took a crying Diane in his arms and held her while his wife did the same with Robin. He was surprised that instead of pulling away, the girls allowed themselves to be held and comforted by strangers and, over the girls' heads, he and his wife exchanged astonished and confused looks. The Marshes held the sobbing girls until all that remained of the hysteria were the hiccups left over.

Peace, at last, Jake thought. Now maybe he could find out what was going on.

"What are your names?" he asked them.

The girls stared at him in disbelief, but for the moment were too tired, too drained, and too confused to start another outburst. They ignored his question and Robin asked again, "Where's Daddy?" The girls started to walk toward the guestroom that was now their father's room, but Jake gently blocked their way.

"I can't help you find your father until you tell me who you are," he said, trying to redirect them back into the living room.

"Grandpa, why are you doing this?" Diane asked, her tone pleading for an answer.

Jake was speechless and looked to his wife for help.

"Something is definitely wrong here," Sarah said to the girls. "You obviously have us confused with someone else—"

"No we don't!" Diane cried. "We know who you are. Why don't you know us?"

"—but we'd like to help you," Sarah continued, ignoring Diane's outburst. "Let's start at the beginning and try to talk this through." She calmly walked toward the kitchen, and the girls numbly followed her, looking at each other blankly.

Sarah spoke softly as she walked, doing her best to be as soothing as possible. "We'll all sit down and put our heads together. Maybe, if we remain calm, we can solve this problem for you." She led them to the table where, hopefully, they would settle down and relax.

At this point, Sarah thought the best thing to do was humor the strangers. "First things first, and please don't get upset that I'm asking. What *are* your names?"

The girls looked at each other with stunned expressions and the same thoughts... *What's going on here? Is this a game of some sort? No, their grandparents wouldn't do this to them. What should they do?* This was worse than being abducted. At least on the alien ship they knew the rules—being scared and in danger was what was *supposed* to happen. Now they were home, and the danger was supposed to be gone. But suddenly, the rules had changed, and they were more scared in a familiar place than they had been in a strange one.

The girls only had one choice for now and, in an unspoken agreement, they decided to follow the new rules as best they could. They each spoke their name in turn.

"Diane."

"Robin."

Sarah nodded in response to each girl, and her husband pulled out a chair for each one. "Please, let's sit down and work this out," she said. As an afterthought, she asked, "Are you hungry? Can I get you something to eat?"

The truth was, the girls were starving, having spent all their efforts on the last leg of their journey, and had not eaten since breakfast. But as hungry as they were, they had no appetite and graciously declined her offer.

"Well, I'll put something out just in case you change your mind." As they all sat down, Sarah put out some fruit, cake, and bread.

Forgetting for the moment these strange circumstances, the girls automatically commented on what they saw being put down. "Wow, you made peanut butter banana bread!" Diane said hungrily, and reached for a piece.

"Boy, did we miss that!" Robin exclaimed, and helped herself to a slice as well.

The older woman stared at the girls, absolutely stunned, and looked at her husband, whose eyes had widened in disbelief. The bread in question was her own secret recipe. She only made it for her husband—her sons didn't like peanut butter—and she had done so just yesterday. How could these girls possibly have known what it was by just looking at it?

"Are you from this area?" inquired the man the girls thought was their grandfather, his curiosity piqued.

"Well… yeah," Robin said, agitation creeping into her voice.

"Where?" Jake asked, trying to keep his voice calm and composed so the girls wouldn't get upset.

"Here!" Diane and Robin answered in unison, unable to believe they were going through this again.

"Where is 'here?'" Jake asked, confused.

"Here, this house!" Diane said, becoming extremely upset once more.

This was going nowhere fast, Jake thought. He tried a

different approach, trying to remain as unruffled as he could. "Do you know anyone else around here?"

"Yes," Robin answered simply, in reply to his query. "Daddy."

Here we go again. "Okay, who is your father?"

Diane remembered an old expression taken from a twentieth-century television show. They had studied the medium in school and had even seen excerpts. The show had been scary in a funny way, but the music haunting. She searched her memory. Something to do with feeling like you were in the…what was it? Oh, yes…"The Twilight Zone." Well, if she never felt that way before, she certainly did now. She looked at Robin and hummed that haunting theme.

"Do you know William Marsh?" Diane asked, feeling silly to be asking such a ridiculous question.

Now we are getting somewhere, Jake Marsh thought, and looked at his wife and smiled. *The girls know Bill, and at least that could be a starting point.*

"Of course we know him. He's our son."

"And he's our father," declared Robin, just as matter-of-factly.

Sarah was shocked by Robin's declaration. "No, that can't be!" cried the woman the girls wanted to be their grandmother.

"But he is!" Diane screamed, and banged her hand on the table, startling everyone. She felt more frustrated than she had ever felt in her entire life. *How do you convince people that they are supposed to know you?*

The girls could tell by the looks on the older couple's faces that they didn't believe a word either of them had said.

"This is so frustrating!" Robin cried. "We are who we say we are! We are!"

"We'll prove it to you," Diane said, not knowing what else to do and feeling desperate. "We can tell you everything about this house."

It didn't really matter what they knew, Jake thought, *they never lived here.* Plain and simple. Information they could have gotten anywhere. But he agreed with his wife that the best thing to do was humor the girls until he could think of something else to do. Making them leave was out of the question. They weren't old enough to be out by themselves, and it was the middle of the night. Tomorrow he would try to find someone who might be able to help them. Tonight, however, Diane and Robin would have to stay here, where at least they would be safe.

The girls took turns rattling off all the details they could think of to try to prove who they were.

Robin started. "This is the house you raised us in until Daddy took us with him. There are three barns in the back."

"The main barn has twenty-eight stalls and all are full," Diane said.

The Marshes let the girls talk and just kept nodding their heads, but had to admit that the accuracy of the details shocked them.

"My horse is the gray one with the black mane, tail, and socks," Diane said.

"And mine is the white one with the most beautiful eyes," Robin chimed in.

They even knew enough to pick the gentlest horses in the barn, Jake thought.

"There are four bedrooms upstairs and a guestroom down here on the main floor. Back there behind the kitchen. That's where Dad stays when he's here," Diane said, pointing in the correct direction of the main-floor guestroom. "You and Grandma have offices behind the living room…over there," she added, again pointing to the correct location.

Robin explained the four bedrooms as the Marshes stared in disbelief. "You and Grandma have the big bedroom that's over the front porch. The bedroom next to yours is another guestroom that has Grandma's collection of old teddy bears." She paused as she remembered the tea parties she and Diane had in that room when they were little girls. The fragile, worn teddy bears had been their playmates and honored guests. "The other two bedrooms were Daddy's and Uncle Brad's."

Both Sarah and Jake flinched when she said "Uncle Brad."

"You know Brad?" Jake asked, shocked.

Diane rolled her eyes. "Of course, he's our uncle. He's a virologist working on Namar II."

This is unbelievable, Jake thought, looking at his wife who had a look of pure amazement on her face. *It's one thing to know they had a son named Brad, but another to know which bedroom he had when growing up. What could these two be up to?*

Robin stopped as she thought of something—a secret she and Diane discovered when they were about four years old. "Dad and Uncle Brad's rooms share a common wall that has a closet on either side. Those closets have a secret passageway between the two rooms." The girls always assumed that their father and uncle put the passageway there, but no one ever mentioned it, so they didn't either. Why would they? They used it to go back and forth when they were supposed to be in their own rooms.

Got them! Jake thought. "No, there is no secret passageway anywhere in this house," he told them victoriously.

"Yes there is!" Diane yelled, emphasizing each word. Then, much more quietly she said, "Please let us show you. Please?" She was practically begging.

The elder two looked at each other in total bewilderment. The faster they got this charade over with, the better.

"Okay, go ahead," Jake said in resignation.

The girls ran up the stairs and into the room at the front of the hallway. The elder couple followed right behind, surprised that the girls never even hesitated to catch their bearings.

Diane was shocked that her room didn't look the same as it did when she left it, but she didn't have time to think of that now. "This is my room and Robin's is next door. Here, look!" she said confidently. She opened the closet and moved the clothes and boxes that were stored there. She got down on her hands and knees and fiddled with the back wall of the closet.

The elder Marshes stood in shock as Diane removed a panel and pushed out one that led to the other room. There it was, as plain as the sun in the sky, a passageway between the rooms. At any other time they might have laughed at their sons' ingenuity, but right now they could only sit down on the bed and stare back and forth between the closet and the girls. No one spoke.

Who were these girls? What on Earth is going on?

"But Bill doesn't have any daughters," Sarah said to her husband, shaking her head in disbelief. "And even if he did, they never lived here with us." She knew she wasn't going crazy. Bill didn't have children. These girls never lived here.

Robin tried to think of the best way to continue, and thought of what their father always said when things got out of hand…*Calm down and start at the beginning. Give me all the details even if you think I already know them.*

"Actually," Robin began, following her father's advice, "we are your son Daniel's daughters." It sounded strange to say those words. Although the girls knew who their biological parents were and spoke about them often with their father, Diane and Robin considered themselves Bill Marsh's daughters. He was the only parent they had ever known, or wanted. She continued her calm explanation. "After he and our mother were killed on Overlan, we lived here on the ranch with you until Daddy could take us with him." It seemed so absurd to be telling them what they should already know.

The elder woman's reaction surprised the girls. At

the sound of the name, Daniel, Sarah started to cry. Her husband put his arm around her and pulled her close, as they both remembered...

Sarah and Jake had met while they were both doing graduate studies at Europa University, which had been built deep beneath the surface of Jupiter's moon, Europa. Sarah was a communications major, specializing in subspace communications, and Jake an engineering major. Her dream was to work on a space station—his dream was to build one. Six months after they graduated, they married. Sarah took a job on Starbase Quadra III and Jake worked as a civilian engineer for Space Central, consulting on numerous space stations being built throughout the galaxy. Shortly after their third wedding anniversary, Sarah was offered a fabulous job on Earth. She had been born and raised on Europa, her parents having emigrated from Earth before her birth. Jake, however, had lived most of his life in New Mexico. The couple moved to Earth and, since Sarah had always wanted an old-fashioned home to raise a family, they found a wonderful ranch in Santa Fe, not far from where Jake had been raised. Within the year, Sarah became pregnant. They were both thrilled and, as soon as they found out their child would be a boy, they picked a name. At the end of four months, Sarah miscarried. "Daniel, my baby," she had cried in her husband's arms, grieving over her lost child.

Even after all the years, the painful memory still hurt like a wound that would not heal. Sarah looked at the two girls and saw the compassion in their eyes as they watched her. She also saw something she could not quite put her finger on—a familiarity to something that kept eluding her. And she knew there was only one way to solve this mystery. She dried her eyes, took a deep breath, and turned to her husband who was still holding her tightly. "Get in touch with Bill," she said. "I don't care how. Use every contact you have in the LUP to find him and bring him home."

"I will," Jake whispered. "I will."

Everything in the house was the same as Diane and Robin had left it, except for their two bedrooms. All their things were gone, as if the girls had never existed. The Marshes offered each girl a bedroom for the night, but the girls wanted to stay in the same room, too afraid to be apart. They chose the one at the top of the stairs, the one that was originally their father's and then Diane's in the home they knew.

Instead of being decorated the way it was just a few days ago, with all of Diane's stuff, it now looked the way it must have looked when their father occupied it. Model spaceships, built by Marsh when he was a boy, hung from the ceiling. Diane stared around the room, speechless. She focused on the spaceship hanging in the corner and nudged Robin to look at it. When the girls were small, they had found the box of model spaceships their grandmother had carefully packed away in the attic. Diane took a fancy to one of the intricately crafted ships, and with her grandfather's help, had hung it back in the same place her father had hung it as a boy. The same corner it was in now.

Unnerved, Diane and Robin crawled into the big bed and tried to fall asleep, but there was no way that sleep would come. Speaking in soft whispers, they tried to grasp what was happening. Over the years, their father had told them all kinds of strange stories about alien races, altered realities, and weird occurrences, so they knew that almost anything was possible. Robin suggested they might still be on the alien ship, drugged and hallucinating this whole ordeal. What was so frightening was that it even made sense. Hours later, exhausted and talked out, they fell asleep, but not before agreeing on one point...*if this wasn't the Twilight Zone, what was?*

CHAPTER 15

NEVER EVEN IN THE REALM OF POSSIBILITY

Contacting his son turned out to be easier than Jake thought it would be. The Polaris was only a few light years from Earth, and he had been able to send a subspace message without any problem. He couldn't give his son too many details, as he didn't understand what was happening himself, but Bill had promised to come and would arrive within the next twenty-four hours.

The sound of the buzzer interrupted Marsh as he was packing a duffel bag for the trip. "Come in."

Gerroll strolled in and got right to the point. "What do you make of the situation, Captain?" he asked, referring to the conversation Marsh had had with his father.

"I don't know, Gerroll. I really don't. But my parents have never once asked me to leave my duties and come home, and I don't think they would have unless it was necessary.

"Ironically, I had thought about calling them and going to visit. This mission of Dr. Wells's doesn't really need my presence, and we are closer to Earth than we've been in a while. But I got caught up here and didn't get a chance. So, now I'll go."

"It's a day-long trip by shuttlecraft," Gerroll reminded him. "Perhaps you could use my assistance." He spoke evenly, hands folded behind his back. His tone was quiet, but his eyes were excited.

As he zipped the bag closed, Marsh turned to look at his second-in-command. "Want to come, Gerroll?" he asked with a grin.

Nodding, Gerroll said, "As you stated, this mission doesn't need your supervision…or mine, for that matter. The bridge crew can easily handle whatever comes. Maybe I could be more assistance to you on Earth. It does sound like an intriguing problem."

"Well, as they say, 'Two heads are better than one.' I'd welcome both your company and your assistance. Go pack your teddy bear and meet on the hangar deck in thirty minutes."

"Teddy bear, Captain?" Gerroll asked, surprised by the captain's comment.

Marsh laughed. "Forget the bear, Gerroll. Just pack some clothes." His mother collected antique teddy bears and had a whole room full of them. Perhaps he could convince her to let Gerroll stay in that room while they were visiting. The thought of Gerroll sleeping surrounded by teddy bears made him smile. The room seemed perfect for his gentle, fun-loving second-in-command.

The elder Marshes decided it was best to remain in limbo until Bill arrived. No discussions or arguments with the girls about who anybody thought the other was. The girls had told them a vague tale about being abducted, but had been reticent to go into much detail. The Marshes didn't want to press the matter, not wanting to upset them more than they already were.

The girls agreed. They were so baffled by what was happening, they also thought it best to wait for him. After all, there wasn't any problem their father couldn't solve. The biggest difficulty for the girls was what to call these people. Obviously, 'Grandma' and 'Grandpa' were out. Calling them 'Mr. and Mrs. Marsh' was too formal to call people who were supposed to be family, and so they settled on calling them nothing at all. It was awkward, but it worked. It was a strange way to exist, but, for now, the best for all concerned.

What was even stranger to the Marshes was how these girls knew their way around. Not just around the ranch, but also around the more intimate places only family usually knew. The girls never asked where anything was, they would just go to the right cabinet to get a glass, the correct drawer for a utensil, and even knew where to find the ever-elusive scissors. It was eerie, and Sarah and Jake were glad when they finally heard the sound of the shuttlecraft landing in the field.

Marsh exited first. He breathed in the smell of the ranch—horses, grass, manure, and hay—all combined into a perfume that was the aroma of his youth, and he realized how much he missed it. He looked at the old ranch house, and the word that came immediately to mind was 'home.' He had come home.

Gerroll looked around, but didn't say anything.

"What's the matter, Gerroll? Nervous about meeting my parents?" Marsh teased.

"No, Captain, but I must admit that I have been very curious."

"About what?" Now Marsh was the curious one.

"Except in a passing reference now and then, you never speak of your family or your home." Gerroll laughed and said jokingly, "I began to think you didn't have one."

Marsh realized what Gerroll said was true. He had met Gerroll's parents, had even become quite familiar with them, and had been to Nimian with his second-in-command on more than one occasion. As captain, Marsh felt he should always maintain a certain distance from his crew. Although he never meant to keep things from Gerroll, who he considered his friend, a very good one at that, Marsh's silence had become natural, and Gerroll never pried, not wanting to cross unspoken boundaries. Despite the odd circumstances, Gerroll was glad for the chance to get a glimpse into his captain's past.

From a distance, Marsh saw his parents exit the house and walk toward them, his mother in the lead.

He spoke with them as often as he could but hadn't seen them in person in a couple of years. It felt good to hug them both, to know they were real and not just computerized images.

Marsh introduced Gerroll, and his parents brought them up to date on the way back to the house, finishing the summary just as they walked through the front door. He looked around and was pleased that little had changed since he left.

"Where are the girls now?" Marsh asked.

"Probably in the barn," his father replied. "They've spent most of their time there, attending to the horses." Jake went on to explain how the girls were so familiar with everything, while his mother fiddled in the kitchen getting them something to eat and drink.

"I just don't know what to make of it," Jake admitted. "But when the girls referred to Daniel, it convinced your mother there's more here than meets the eye. I can't say that I disagree with her."

"They are really nice, sweet girls—bright, cheerful, and actually a lot of fun. They just don't seem the type to pull an elaborate hoax," his mother added.

"By the way," his father interrupted, changing the subject, "just when did you and Brad put that passageway in the closet?"

Marsh laughed at the memory. "Remember the time we let all the horses out of the corral to see how far they would run, and then you sent us to our rooms for the remainder of the weekend? Well, we got bored sitting there! We were never sure whether or not you knew about it!"

"Trust me, son, if I had known, you wouldn't be laughing," his father said sternly, but was chuckling as he said it.

His mother came over to the table and stood next to her husband. "I'm serious, Bill. They *are* nice girls. I don't know what's happening, but whoever they are, they must be scared to death."

"Your mother is correct, Captain," Gerroll said. "Perhaps it's time we should meet them."

"Any ideas, Gerroll?"

"I do have a theory, Captain, but I need to see them."

They couldn't have asked for better timing. The kitchen door opened and the two girls walked in, slightly disheveled and smelling of horses. They had been talking to each other, but stopped when they realized there were people in the room. Then they saw Marsh and without thinking they yelled, "Daddy!" and ran toward him. Shocked, Marsh took a step back and the girls, seeing his reaction, stopped in their tracks as they remembered the reality of their current situation. But they couldn't take their eyes off him.

How could this man not be our father? the sisters wondered, heartbroken and speechless.

Sarah came to the rescue. She nodded at each girl as she said her name.

"Diane. Robin…" she began and then hesitated. "This is my son…"

"Bill Marsh," Robin said softly, barely able to get the words out. "Yes, we know." Tears were stinging her eyes, and she didn't need to look at Diane to know exactly what her sister was feeling.

The girls had discussed the situation at length and decided, at least for now, no one knew who they were. They didn't know why and could only guess that something horrible and unexplainable must have happened while they were away. Hopefully, they could piece it together as time went on.

"Hi, Gerroll," Diane said, not waiting for, or needing, an introduction.

"You know me?" he asked, surprised but delighted.

She sighed, tired of trying to prove who she was. "Yes. You're the second-in-command on the Polaris and also Da...my fath...his friend," she said pointing to Marsh.

"I like them already," Gerroll said, smiling broadly at the two scared girls.

For a brief second, everyone stood in silence just staring at one another, feeling very uncomfortable. Gerroll spoke first. "Captain, may I speak to you in private for a moment?"

"Sure, Gerroll," Marsh said, glad for the reprieve. He maneuvered his second-in-command into the guestroom. "What are you thinking?"

"As I mentioned earlier, I do have a theory, but in order to prove it I would like to use my telepathic abilities, if that is okay with you."

"Absolutely...of course...whatever you think will

help solve this mystery. Do you want to sit with them at the same time?"

"No, I believe separately would be best. Perceptions of the same event are experienced differently by different people, and I would like as much information as I can get."

"I understand."

"And Bill, I'd like you to stay. I think your presence will help."

Marsh wasn't so sure about that, but would go along with whatever Gerroll suggested. "Okay. You seem to feel confident about this." He left for only a few seconds and returned with Robin.

"Gerroll is going to try and help us get to the bottom of this. Please cooperate with him and do what he says," Marsh told her. Then he sat down on the bed and tried to remain as unobtrusive as possible.

Robin nodded her head. "I will." She seemed at ease with both of them, and didn't flinch when Gerroll approached her.

Gerroll took both of her hands in his…he didn't need physical contact to use his telepathic abilities, but he sensed she needed the comfort. "Think of home," he told her, his voice a soft, gentle whisper. "Focus, Robin. Think of the events that brought you here." She was scared, but she trusted him.

While Robin was concentrating, Gerroll sought the memories he needed, but was bombarded by her feelings of confusion, loneliness, and fright. He saw her sister and felt the bond they shared. He felt her overwhelming need for the man she called her father, and the image in her mind was that of the man he saw everyday on the bridge of the Polaris. The similarities he saw shocked him. He sensed the shadows of those that no longer existed but had given them life…and he understood the loss she felt for having never known them. Robin tried to block her thoughts of the events that had taken her from the safety of her world—they were too painful to remember—and Gerroll had to go deeper to draw them out. She resisted his effort, but she was no match for his abilities, and he found what he was looking for.

"What's taking so long?" Diane asked nervously. She had begun to pace the room.

"I don't know," said the man who was, but wasn't, her grandfather. "I'm sure they will be back soon. Sit down, Diane, and relax for a few minutes." He patted the couch where both he and his wife were already sitting.

"I can't," she said and continued her walking tour of the room.

"What is it, Gerroll?" Marsh asked. Gerroll had finished the first telepathic bond and was deep in thought, looking out of the window and into the field.

"A few more minutes, Captain. Please bring Diane in."

Marsh didn't question him any further. He knew that, although Gerroll loved fun and games, when he got down to work, he focused totally on his task and didn't like to be disturbed until he had finished.

"You did fine," Marsh told Robin. He brought her back into the living room and motioned for Diane to follow him.

His parents watched him, hoping for an answer, but got none.

"Sit and relax, Robin," they prompted, once Bill and Diane disappeared into the other room.

Robin sat on the couch, leaned back, and closed her eyes, drained from the experience. *Please have the answers,* she thought. *I can't go on like this much longer.*

Diane gave her full trust to Gerroll, as her sister had, but this time he understood why. Their Gerroll was an important part of their lives—they had known him since they were little—and they trusted him implicitly. It was interesting to read her perceptions of him. Her emotions flooded him; she was more scared than she let on. The images in her mind were of people he thought he should know, and it was discomforting to see them there, familiar and unfamiliar at the same time, especially those of her father. She, too, resisted his efforts to discover what had happened to her, as if thinking about it would force the reality of something she so desperately wanted to deny. But, as with her sister, he found what he needed and, in doing so, he found the answers to his questions.

It wasn't a long wait. Within minutes, Diane rejoined them in the living room. Marsh squeezed her shoulder in reassurance and held up a finger to his parents, indicating that they should be patient and wait a few more minutes while he went back to talk with Gerroll.

Diane joined Robin on the couch, equally exhausted. There was no need for words; their hopes were the same.

Marsh looked at Gerroll with both hands held out, eager for an explanation. "Well, Gerroll?"

"It's just as I thought, Bill," Gerroll said and laughed. "You're not going to believe this…"

When they returned, Marsh asked them all to sit around the kitchen table. Talking mainly to the girls, he said, "Gerroll has something to explain to you, and I want you to listen to him very, very carefully."

Gerroll leaned forward and tried to choose the words that, though not entirely scientific, would best illustrate the situation for the girls. "I had formulated a theory before I met you, and it was confirmed. When you were abducted, you were taken from your universe into our universe."

"Another *universe*," Robin asked incredulously, her eyes as wide as saucers. She looked at her sister to make sure Diane had heard the same thing. Diane returned her look, shocked and speechless.

"Yes," Gerroll confirmed. "Another universe that coexists in space and time with yours. Almost identical. Almost, but not completely. That is why everything here is so familiar to you, but slightly altered. You see," he hesitated, not sure how they would handle the next piece of information, "in this universe, Daniel was not born, and neither were you."

Diane and Robin stared at Gerroll, and then at each person sitting around the table, trying desperately to assimilate the information that they just heard. "And since Daniel wasn't born," Diane reiterated, speaking very slowly as she got her thoughts together, "you never became our father," she said, motioning in Marsh's direction, "and you were never our grandparents," she said as she looked at the two older Marshes. "That explains why you don't know us but we know you. Everything else, more or less, remains the same. Is that right?"

"Exactly," Gerroll confirmed for her.

It was a lot to digest at one time. The girls hadn't known what to think, had thrown around a lot of ideas, but this was never even in the realm of possibility.

"Our life, our world, is someplace else," Robin said, her voice barely a whisper. "No one we know…our father doesn't exist here. At least not as we know him."

"No, but we are here." It was the soft soothing voice of their grandmother. Her heart ached for them. Everyone and everything they had known was suddenly out of reach. "As long as you are in this universe we *are* your family, and you can treat us that way. From now on, I *am* 'Grandma.'" Those weren't empty words she spoke merely to make the girls feel better. She meant every single one of them. The explanation had astonished her as much as it had the girls. But Daniel *had* existed within her for a brief time, and these were the children he would have had if circumstances had been different. These girls were a part of him, and he had been a part of her. For all intents and purposes, she *was* their grandmother—as real as their grandmother in their own universe.

"And I am 'Grandpa,'" Jake said to them.

The girls smiled at them but sat very still, trying to absorb their new world. They looked at Marsh. It was hard to look at him now. It hurt too much. He wasn't who they wanted or needed him to be.

"What should we call *you*?" Robin asked him, finding it difficult to keep her voice from trembling.

He didn't give an answer because he couldn't think of one. Again, his mother rescued him.

"How about 'Uncle Bill?'" Sarah suggested to him. "Technically, it's what you are in their world."

Marsh nodded numbly, aware that somehow he also had to fit into this altered equation.

Sarah looked at her new granddaughters and smiled. "Would that be okay?"

"It's better than 'Hey, you,'" Diane said. Everyone laughed, although she hadn't meant to be funny. How could they possibly look at this man and call him anything but "Daddy?"

Marsh never doubted the existence of parallel universes, but this was his first proof. The mystique of the universe had always held him in awe, and it was the main driving force that had pushed him to explore it. He wanted to find the answers to the questions people have been asking since the beginning of time, every time they looked up into the night sky and saw the tiny blinking lights. *What lies within the folds of the fabric of the never-ending universe?* He wondered it too. He thought of the explanation that Gerroll had given Diane and Robin—different universes that coexist within the same time and space as ours…within the folds of the fabric.

Marsh knew there were numerous theories for the existence of parallel universes. Scientists theorize that there could be an infinite number of universes, and that each one of us might have an infinite number of counterparts coexisting at the same time—a thought almost too intense to comprehend. The theories go on to say that these counterparts are not exactly the same, and that each universe has been slightly altered by an event that occurs in one universe, but not another. In this case, it was the birth of an older brother that happened in the girls' universe, but not this one.

He couldn't help but think of his counterpart in Diane and Robin's universe—a starship captain with two daughters. He shook his head. To him, it was an absolutely ridiculous and inconceivable notion. In this universe, commanders were not even allowed to have their own children aboard, and he agreed with that rule. He wondered what had happened in the girls' universe that had changed that policy. Then a thought struck him…*was it because of his counterpart that the rule had been changed? Could that be? Were these two girls responsible for Space Central's reversal of this policy in their universe?*

There were one hundred ninety-two children on the Polaris, but Marsh very rarely interacted with them, except for Jared, who was the son of Matt and Kate Wells. The thought of having children never occurred to him. Still, he couldn't stop his thoughts from continuing to…"What if"…

No. For him, the universes were so far apart there couldn't possibly be a "what if." Yet, the thought nagged at him.

It was agreed they would stay for a few more days before bringing the girls back to the Polaris. This would give them all a chance to get to know one another better in a comfortable and familiar environment, and give Marsh and Gerroll some time to strategize.

They spent a quiet evening together, but the girls were drained, sad, and understandably confused. Marsh tried to question them over dinner about the abduction, but didn't get far, and heeded his mother's looks to leave them alone.

Diane and Robin went to bed early, and Sarah went with them, trying to comfort them as best she could. At least they finally understood what had happened and, for the first time in days, they went to sleep knowing that the morning would bring a world they could comprehend.

CHAPTER 16

BUT HE LOOKS LIKE DAD

Diane and Robin were early risers. On the ranch at home that meant they could get in a ride before breakfast, and that is just where they headed. They were surprised to find Marsh already there, saddling his horse. He was more startled to see *them*. He had been looking forward to a quiet morning ride by himself to help get his still unresolved feelings in order. There was suddenly so much to think about—and so much he didn't understand.

"Good morning, Uncle Bill," Diane said cheerfully, but the words didn't roll off her tongue easily. The sisters were still uneasy in his presence, not sure how he would react to them.

"Good morning, girls," he responded in a polite but stiff voice. They made him uncomfortable, and he wondered what to talk about, an unusual occurrence for him. His diplomatic training usually took over and got him through most situations smoothly. But not this one. No training in the world was going to help him here.

His parents were completely at ease with the girls. They picked up the role of grandparents as if they had been waiting their whole lives for this and Marsh could tell they were enjoying it, especially his mother. It had been a long time since she had anyone to dote on, except his father, and Marsh was glad she was happy. Yet, he was unsettled. For some reason he felt that *he* was the one that didn't belong. That he was supposed to be someone else and that something was expected of him that he was not capable of giving.

"We're going riding this morning," Robin told him while she and Diane started to get their equipment together.

"No, you're not," he said as he tightened the cinch on the saddle.

The girls stopped what they were doing and looked at him, dumbfounded. "Why not?" Diane questioned.

"It's not safe. Gerroll and I—"

"That's ridiculous!" Diane yelled, not even attempting to hide her annoyance or let him finish his sentence. "We ride alone all the time!"

"That's not what I meant, and don't raise your voice to me, young lady," he chastised her, in a tone too much like their father's. The sisters were taken aback, but only for a second.

Marsh tried to remain calm and explain his decision.

"We haven't determined yet why you were abducted, and we can't be sure someone isn't still looking for you. As a matter of fact, you are not allowed to be by yourself at all from now on." He started to lead his horse from the barn, but the girls continued the dispute.

"But we've been riding alone for two days *before* you came and nothing's happened," Robin argued, trying hard to keep her voice low while she tried to reason with him. Unfortunately, she wasn't succeeding, and the more agitated she became, the more annoyed he got. She couldn't help it—he was so frustrating, so stubborn.

"Well, that's going to change," he told them bluntly. He wasn't used to his orders being questioned and was quickly losing patience, even though he knew he should be more tolerant. "It's for your own safety, and I don't want to hear any more about it. Go back into the house and we'll talk about it later."

Diane and Robin looked at each other and then back at him. No way were they going back into the house.

He saw another argument coming and nipped it in the bud. "Or, you can spend the rest of the day in your room." He knew that was totally uncalled for—he shouldn't have said it. His reaction perplexed him, but they brought out something in him he just didn't understand and couldn't seem to get a handle on.

"You've got to be kidding," Diane said in disbelief. "That's not fair." She could feel the tears of frustration beginning to sting her eyes, but would be damned if she'd let *him* see them.

She was right, it wasn't fair, he thought. He was just about to apologize when Diane asked, "Can we ride with you?"

Diane got one of Robin's "you've got to be kidding" looks, shrugged at her in response, and waited for Marsh to answer.

Marsh sighed inwardly, but knew he had to get over this awkward feeling that was beginning to overwhelm him. Maybe a morning ride with them would be a good idea. "Okay. Groom the horses first and then saddle up. Don't give them any food—they ate earlier. If you need help, call me."

"We *know* what to do," Diane told him, her tone clipped.

"Good, then do it," he countered, his tone equally clipped. He led his horse outside without giving them another glance.

Robin stood and glared at her sister, and in the most sarcastic voice she could muster said, "Good going, Diane. This is going to be a fun morning."

"I didn't know what else to do. I blurted out the first thing I could think of. I'm sorry, Rob."

They looked out into the yard and watched Marsh mount his horse. From afar, they couldn't tell the difference between him and their father. The difference up close, however, was beyond measure.

Diane watched him and sighed, seeing him, but wanting her father. "Let's give him a chance, Rob. Dad's got to be in there somewhere."

"Are you sure?"

They both continued to watch him.

Diane shook her head sadly, the tears she was holding back finally falling. "No," she whispered, "No, I'm not."

They rode in silence until they came to a fork in the road. Diane turned to her sister, smiled playfully, and then said to Marsh, "Why don't we go that way?" She pointed toward the right and tried to look as innocent as she could.

Robin shook her head in disbelief. She knew exactly what her *father* would say to that question. She could hear his tone and could even picture him saying it. She was surprised her sister would even try to test this man, but waited to hear his response, nonetheless.

Diane also knew what her father would say. She remembered, only too well, what had happened last summer…

As much as the girls loved living on the Polaris, summer vacation was special. It was the time that they got to spend with their grandparents on the ranch, visit old friends and, of course, be with Pepper and Cloud. Jared came home, too, and stayed with his grandparents at the neighboring ranch. The three children were usually inseparable, spending long, lazy days riding and relaxing, enjoying the real sunshine instead of the simulated light on the ship.

Marsh was able to take shore leave and joined his daughters for a couple of weeks toward the end of the summer, although he didn't see much of them. They were out most of the time enjoying what was left of their vacation, and he got a chance to relax and take some time for himself, a very rare occurrence on the Polaris.

His parents were spending this particular day in town and had asked the girls to go with them. Robin wanted to go because they were passing a store she had been meaning to get to all summer, but Diane declined, saying she wanted to stay home alone and maybe go riding by herself.

Marsh was going to visit Mr. and Mrs. Kingston, old friends of the family who had a ranch a few miles north of his parents'. The Kingston's youngest son, Robert, was stationed on Starbase 4B. When the Polaris had a layover there a few weeks earlier, Marsh had gotten together with Robert for dinner. He thought it would be nice to let the Kingstons know that he had seen their son and all was well.

He met Diane on his way to the barn and they fell into stride together. "I'm going over to the Kingston's to say hello. I shouldn't be there long. Afterwards, I'm going to take a ride, but I will be home by dinner. Why don't you come with me?"

"No thanks, Dad," she said, shaking her head.

This was the first time Marsh could ever remember Diane turning down a ride with him. "What are you going to do here all day by yourself?"

"Don't know. I haven't decided yet. Maybe take a ride myself later." She leaned against the rim of the open barn door and watched as her father got his horse, Starry Night, and prepared him for the afternoon ride. When his horse was tacked and ready, he tried again. "Are you sure you don't want to come?"

"Yeah," she replied, not moving from her spot against the barn door.

Still surprised by his daughter's decision he said, "I have my communication badge, so contact me at the Kingston's if you change your mind. I'll ride back and get you. Make sure you take your badge if you go out riding by yourself. And don't go too far."

"Yeah, okay Dad."

After mounting his horse, he took a few strides so he was next to his daughter. "And Diane…" he said, and waited to make sure he had her attention.

She squinted as she looked up at him, the sun directly behind his head. "What?"

"Remember what we talked about."

"Goodbye, Dad. Have a nice afternoon," she said curtly as she walked away from him and into the barn.

He let her sarcasm slide, knowing he had touched a sore topic.

Go already, she thought, as she began to get her stuff together for her ride. She threw the saddle down on the ground in anger as she remembered their little "talk." A cloud of dust rose from the barn floor and settled onto the black leather saddle and her shoes. It hadn't been a mutual conversation. Her father had talked, and she listened, frustrated and annoyed.

Twice so far, her father had discovered that she'd been riding to places where she wasn't allowed to ride, because he *had* decided they were too dangerous. He flat out told her that if she did it again he would take Pepper away from her. He said that if she couldn't be responsible enough *to ride in safe places for Pepper's safety, then she couldn't have him.*

Fred Blake, a friend of her grandfather's, had asked if he could borrow either Pepper or Cloud to teach his visiting granddaughter to ride. They were the gentlest of horses and would be perfect for the job.

"One more time," her father had warned her, "and I will send Pepper to Fred Blake's for the remainder of the summer, and you will not ride at all."

She had been furious. Pepper was her *horse, and as long as she was around, no one would ride him but her. Besides, it was ridiculous because she always rode slowly and carefully if she thought it might be dangerous. Her father was just too stubborn to see that she could handle it.*

When he was finally gone, she saddled Pepper. It was a beautiful day to ride, and she packed snacks and water so she could stay out all afternoon, but defiantly pulled off her communication badge, which she usually wore as a pendant around her neck, and threw it onto the straw in Pepper's stall.

Trotting slowly along the path that led from the ranch, she admired the acres of soft grass on either side and the beautiful mountains of Santa Fe all around. Then she let Pepper settle into a smooth, comfortable canter. She rode about a mile or so up the road and then stopped to look around.

Her thought when she set out was to go to the creek and spend the afternoon reading under a tree. But standing at the fork in the road, she changed her mind. She would go into the hills instead. It was where she was forbidden to go, but there was no one around to see her. She'd been there before and, despite what her father thought, she knew she wouldn't have any problems.

The afternoon went quickly and Diane didn't venture too far off course, staying only where she knew her way. In places where the path became too steep or rocky, she dismounted and led Pepper by the reins, always making sure that he was safe. She wished her father could see her and realize that she was responsible.

Quite by chance, she found a tiny clearing, a private little alcove surrounded by trees, and thick with grass and leaves. She spread her blanket out on the ground, sat against one of the trees, and read for a couple of hours while Pepper grazed and cooled down.

It was getting late and she had to be home in time for dinner. Still having a long ride ahead of her, she packed up and headed back to the ranch. A shortcut she had found on one of her forbidden afternoon jaunts was close by, and she decided to take that path to save some time. After riding for about fifteen minutes, she found the trail blocked by a huge, fallen tree that was too big for Pepper to cross. The terrain on her right was too steep for either herself or Pepper to climb. She looked over to her left… and down. Actually, that wasn't too bad, she thought. It wasn't very steep, and at the bottom was a stream that was almost dried up. She even knew how to get home from there. It was her only choice. If she turned around, she would never make it home in time for dinner and there would be too many questions to answer. She dismounted and began to lead Pepper down the hill. Halfway down, *she stumbled and slid the rest of the way. She landed in the mud, which was all that was left of the stream and much deeper than she thought it would be. She looked up and watched Pepper clumsily making his way down the slippery hill. He'd almost made it to the bottom, but then he, too, lost his balance and slid into the muddy stream. Diane couldn't help but laugh. What a sight they were! At least Pepper seemed to be enjoying himself. He was rolling around in the mud as if the stream was his own private playpen.*

She tried to get up, but the mud was so thick it took three attempts before she could even stand, each attempt ending with her seated back in the mud. Finally, she toppled on to the dry shore of the creek and waited for Pepper to get up while she tried to clean herself off. She hoped Pepper was having a good time—it would take her forever to clean him up and she'd have to ride him home covered in mud.

But something was wrong. Pepper was on his back, but not rolling over. She got up to take a closer look and realized, with horror, what had happened. The thick mud was acting like a suction cup—his saddle was caught and being held in it! He couldn't break free and couldn't get up. Horses spook easily and Pepper was definitely spooked. His legs were flailing wildly and he was flipping his head back and forth. The harder he tried to get up and couldn't, the more spooked he got.

Diane tried to help him, but he was one thousand pounds of uncontrollable horse and she couldn't budge him. She didn't have her communication badge, and so she did the only thing she could think of—she screamed and screamed and screamed.

Luckily, two of the ranch hands, Max and Carl, were checking the electronic fences on the northern rim of the ranch. They heard Diane's screams and rode over as fast as they could. When they were satisfied that she was okay, they went to help poor Pepper.

But Max and Carl weren't the only ones who heard her scream—they were just closer. Marsh had been on his way home when Diane's screams cut the silence. By the time he got there, things were under control, and Max and Carl were helping Pepper stand.

Transfixed by the scene in front of her, Diane never saw her father ride up. Marsh didn't dismount, but instead watched his daughter watch her horse, a look of sheer terror on her face. He didn't have all of the details yet, but could pretty much guess what had transpired.

When Pepper was up and okay and her gaze broken, Diane looked up and saw him sitting there. She had no idea how long he'd been there, and she felt the blood drain from her face.

"Thank you," Marsh said to Max and Carl, never taking his eyes off his daughter. "You saved Pepper from an uncertain fate. Please take him back to the barn. Diane will clean him off when she gets back."

His left foot slid from the stirrup to make room for hers, and he held his hand out to her, indicating that she should mount and ride with him on the back of his horse. She did so without question. He rode slowly all the way back to the barn so as not to jostle her too much, and she held him securely around his waist, her head resting on his back. Neither spoke.

When they finally made it back to the ranch, he flipped his right foot over the horn of the saddle, jumped down, and caught her as she slid off the rump of the horse. Still holding her by the shoulders, Marsh gave his daughter her instructions.

"Give Pepper a bath, groom him, feed him, and put him away for the night. Then clean off his saddle. When you are through with that, go inside, get yourself cleaned up, and come down for dinner. We will talk about this later. Understand?"

"Yes, Sir," she said, nodding, but not meeting her father's gaze.

Marsh commanded a starship—almost everyone in the galaxy called him "Sir," and he never thought twice about it. But this was the first time he'd ever heard one of his children call him that. Suddenly, it sounded cold and impersonal, and he didn't like it. He didn't correct her, though—he understood why she said it. She was scared of what he was going to do, and she had every right to be.

Now he had a very hard decision to make.

Diane watched her father walk back into the house and then did everything he had told her to do. Not that obeying him now would help, but she did not want to make her predicament any worse.

She enjoyed Pepper's bath almost as much as Pepper did. They were both hot and caked with mud, and the cool water felt refreshing. When he was nice and clean, Diane spent a long time grooming him. He'd been so good all day and he deserved the pampering. She petted him and kissed him on the soft, velvety spot between his nostrils—made just for kissing. Then she buried her head in his newly combed and untangled mane and cried. There was no doubt in her mind he would be gone in the morning.

Diane went into the house to clean up and get ready for dinner, but was frustrated because she couldn't find Robin. Where was she? She needed to talk with her sister, to tell her what happened and get her advice, but Robin was nowhere to be found and didn't appear until they were all seated at the dinner table. She had been in the backyard reading a new book she had picked up that afternoon in town, and oblivious to her sister's search for her.

Looking carefully around the table to check for reactions, Diane wondered if her father had told her grandparents what had happened. No one mentioned it and the conversation seemed the same as usual. Even though she was sitting right across from her sister, Diane couldn't say anything about the events of the day.

But Robin sensed something was wrong. Diane had barely said a word and was moving the food around on her plate instead of eating it, which was odd because they both loved their grandmother's home-cooked meals, an unusual treat in a world of automated food dispensers and nutritional supplements. Diane's eyes kept trying to tell her something and Robin could only guess that it wasn't good news.

When dinner was over, Marsh addressed his older daughter. "Diane, what you did today affects the entire family. Although Pepper is your horse, he is, in his own way, a member of this family. His fate is everyone's concern. Tell us exactly what happened this afternoon."

Not looking at anyone but Robin, Diane hesitantly gave all the details. It was easy to tell Robin anything, but she couldn't face the rest of the family. Poor Robin, hearing this for the first time and trying to remain calm. She knew what was going to happen and how her sister would react.

"What did I tell you would happen if you disobeyed me?" Marsh asked when Diane had finished her saga.

"You'd take Pepper away from me," she answered nonchalantly, trying to say the words as if they were just words with no true meaning or substance, while her real feelings bubbled underneath. When her father nodded in affirmation, she realized that he really might do it, despite her absolute refusal to believe it. No, this can't happen. It can't, *she thought. Her heart was suddenly in her mouth, and the tears she didn't want anybody to see were streaming down her cheeks. "Daddy, please don't take Pepper away from me." She was pleading with him, and the words were almost inaudible through her tears.*

Marsh repeated the words to himself..."Daddy, please." Two little words that had the power to cause him so much pleasure...or grief. Sometimes it was easy to grant his daughters' requests and make them happy, and sometimes, like tonight, it wasn't. He wished he could always give them what they wanted, but knew it wasn't possible.

"You don't want me to take Pepper away from you?"

"N...n...n...no." It came out in a series of staccato syllables as she tried to catch her breath through the tears.

"You have twenty-four hours."

She looked at him quizzically, not understanding what he meant, but cognizant of the fact that he had given her some sort of reprieve.

Marsh continued his explanation. "By tomorrow evening, you will have an essay prepared to read for me. Hand-written. It will cover the following subjects...what you did today and why, the reasons I shouldn't take Pepper away from you, and what your punishment should be for what happened today. What you write will determine Pepper's fate." He paused to give her a chance to absorb the instructions and then asked, "Do you understand what you have to do?"

"Yes," she said, nodding her head excitedly, thankful for the chance to keep her horse.

"Okay then, until tomorrow night."

She got up to leave, but turned back. "Thank you, Daddy."

"Don't thank me yet. Your task is more difficult than you think."

So relieved that her father hadn't sent Pepper away, at least not yet, Diane didn't even think about the essay until the morning. It wasn't until she sat down to write that she realized how hard it was going to be. She must have thrown away a few dozen sheets of paper and still couldn't get the first sentence correct. Her father had taken Robin out for the day—on purpose, she was sure. With no one to help, she began to think she wouldn't be able to get it done, and even if she did, it wouldn't be acceptable and her father would send Pepper away for the remainder of the summer. Panic was beginning to set in, and she decided to put the essay away for a while. She lay down on her bed and closed her eyes, going over the events of yesterday in her head. She fell asleep, and when she woke up, she realized that she only had a couple of hours until dinner. But the nap had cleared her mind and helped her to think straight.

The sisters met on the stairs on the way down to dinner. "Rob, did Dad say anything about Pepper today?" Diane asked, and waited expectantly for the answer.

Robin shook her head slowly, sorry she couldn't help. "Nope. Not a word."

"Oh." Diane was disappointed. She'd hoped her father might drop some sort of clue to Robin about what he was thinking. "What did you two do all day?"

"Dad wanted to look at some horses that were for sale over at Duncan Farm. We could have taken the hovercar, but he wanted to take the horses instead. I think he wanted me gone as long as possible so I couldn't help you." She felt so bad for her sister. "You okay?"

Diane shrugged. "I don't know. I guess so. Depends on what happens tonight." She stopped as they reached the bottom of the stairs and looked at her sister. "Rob, what am I going to do if he takes Pepper away from me?"

"Don't worry," Robin said as confidently as she could. "I'm sure he'll let you keep him." Then she added what they both knew to be true, "But he won't make it easy…you can count on that!" She smiled her best smile of encouragement and squeezed her sister's arm.

Grimacing, Diane looked at her sister and nodded, knowing what Robin said was true. "No, he won't make it easy. But if he lets Pepper stay, then it will be worth it."

Dinner went much too quickly and Diane wasn't sure she was ready to read what she had written. What if it wasn't good enough and he sent Pepper away?

"You have something to read, Diane?" Marsh asked when the girls had finished clearing the dishes.

"Yes," she said, looking around the table, trying to find the confidence she didn't feel. She caught Robin's eye and Robin grinned at her, giving her the encouragement she needed.

"Go ahead," he said softly. He knew this was difficult for her, but he also knew that both she and Pepper could have been seriously injured by her actions yesterday.

Diane pulled out the page, took a deep breath, and started to read. "Daddy," the essay started. The words were really for him and no one else, although they would all hear them. "You told me to start with what I did yesterday and why. You already know the events—I gave them to you at dinner last night. The details aren't important. What I really did was disobey you, disappoint you, and cause you to lose trust in me. I don't know why I did it except that I thought I could. I thought I knew better than you and that you were wrong. But, you weren't wrong, I was." She was already fighting back tears, but was determined to get through this without crying. Her voice, however, was tentative and shaky.

"I love Pepper, Daddy, and that's the only reason I could think of for why you shouldn't take him away from

me. I promise…I swear…never to do anything that might be harmful to him. I will be responsible and keep him safe. I will. I really will. Please give me another chance."

She looked up and saw her father watching her intently, but his face didn't give her any hint of what he was thinking or how she was doing. She spoke to him, uncomfortable by what she was going to ask. "Daddy, the next part was really, really hard." She paused and swallowed. "Do you think that maybe you could come up with the punishment instead of me? You're so good at it since you've had so much practice." She smiled at him, trying hard to break the tension.

Marsh did his best to hide the smile that was trying to escape, aware that his parents were looking away in an effort to cover their own grins. He didn't say anything. He couldn't. He knew if he opened his mouth, he would laugh, so he just shook his head to indicate that no, she would have to do as she was told.

"Oh well, it was worth a try," she said, and went back to reading. "I knew you'd make me do this. Having to come up with one's own punishment is punishment in itself. I guess that's why I have to do it." She looked at her father and he nodded, glad that she understood.

"I tried to think of what you would do, of all the punishments you've given us." She looked at Robin who shook her head and smiled. "Robin would say, 'Be creative'…like you always are. Like this is." She waved her hand in an expansive gesture around the table, letting him know that she considered this lesson creative. "But I racked my brain all day and couldn't come up with anything."

Marsh smiled to himself. His daughters teased him about his lessons being "creative" because he tried to fit the punishment to what they had done, oftentimes coming up with penalties that surprised them.

She hadn't written anything more on this subject, figuring she'd feel her way through it. She looked at her father and asked, "How about one week of no privileges including, of course, not riding Pepper, and extra chores around the house?"

Marsh smiled but was shaking his head no. Not good enough.

"Two weeks?" *she bargained.*

He was still shaking his head, but he wasn't smiling anymore.

He really is making this hard, Diane thought. *She took a deep breath and said,* "Okay, two weeks of no privileges, no riding, extra chores, and I'll muck out all the stalls every day."

Her father was looking at her, no longer shaking his head, but not nodding, either. Just watching her.

What does he want from me? *she wondered, exasperated. She just didn't know, and she felt as if Pepper was slipping away from her. It was precisely that thought that made her realize what he expected. She stared at him with a look of such sorrow he knew she had figured it out.*

Diane sighed a sigh filled with resignation and sadness. "Plus," she said, "I'll lend Pepper to Mr. Blake for two weeks so he can teach his granddaughter to ride," *then quickly added,* "but he'll be back before we leave so I can ride him…safely and responsibly, of course."

THE CAPTAIN'S DAUGHTERS

Finally, he nodded.

The girls waited to see what Uncle Bill would say to Diane's suggestion to ride into the hills.

"No, the terrain's too dangerous. You're not allowed up there under any circumstances. Understand?" Marsh answered, his voice adamant.

Diane nodded at him to let him know she understood, and then leaned over to Robin and whispered, "Maybe there's hope yet."

Robin nodded and stared at this Bill Marsh. Same words, same tone, even the same inflections as their father. *Scary*, she thought.

"I have a favorite spot," he told them. "I'll take you there instead."

"The waterfall behind the creek?" Robin said. It was a statement and question at the same time. *Maybe, just maybe, Diane was right and there was some hope for him after all,* she thought.

"Yes, how did you—" But he knew the answer before the question was out of his mouth. "Your father's favorite place?"

The girls smiled and nodded.

This is definitely unnerving, he thought, and headed for the creek. He was impressed with their riding and told them so.

"Dad taught us when we were small, while we still lived on the ranch with Grandma and Grandpa. Before we went to live with him," Robin explained.

"He did a good job," Marsh said, and meant it.

They were good riding partners. They anticipated his moves and kept up nicely.

When they got to the creek, they pointed out where, on their Earth, they had been abducted—but wouldn't talk about it. They skillfully dodged his questions, just as they had done the night before. He didn't push them. When they felt more secure with him, he was sure they would open up.

They dismounted, tied the horses, and followed the trail around the creek and into the woods. The path was wet and slippery, but they took it slowly, walking silently through the fallen, soggy leaves. The sun peaked through the tops of the trees, sending streaks of warm, morning sunlight down at them. They had to walk across a bridge made from a fallen tree, which passed over the creek. More than once when he was young, Marsh had either slipped or purposely jumped into the cool waters below. Today, however, he carefully watched his steps and those of the two girls in his care. When they had made it safely to the other side, they could hear the rush of the waterfall. Just a few more steps around the bend and they were rewarded with the spectacular view of water cascading from the rocks above, and the rainbows that were cast when the sun shone on the glistening mist.

Marsh had seen beautiful sights on dozens of exotic planets, but this place from his childhood remained his favorite. "Do you come here with your father?" he asked quietly.

They both nodded.

"You miss him?" He probably shouldn't have asked but did anyway, not quite sure why. Maybe it was the way they looked so sadly at the waterfall.

Neither girl answered for a while. They both stood, as he did, absorbed in the tranquility of the view.

Diane turned to him. A tear rolled down her cheek, and she quickly brushed it away. "Can you get us home to him?" she asked, her voice a mere whisper.

Her question answered his, but he didn't know how to answer hers.

CHAPTER 17

WHAT IF...

BREAKFAST WAS WAITING for them when they returned to the ranch. *My mother is really enjoying this*, Marsh thought as he surveyed the spread on the table. She had made all of his favorites.

After breakfast, he and Gerroll went off to talk, but not before he leaned down to give his mother a kiss on the cheek to thank her for the fabulous meal. His father went to do an inspection of the ranch, and the ladies remained in the kitchen, still sitting around the table.

Sarah couldn't hold back her curiosity any longer. "What's your father like?" she asked the girls. She'd been trying to imagine her Bill with two daughters, aboard the Polaris, no less, but couldn't do it. He had a formality about him that just didn't lend itself to children, let alone daughters.

She hoped the girls would want to talk about their father, not just to satisfy her curiosity, but also to let out the emotions she was sure they were keeping in. They must miss him terribly.

She was right. They started talking at once, filling her with stories about their lives with their Bill Marsh. In many ways, he was so much like her son.

"Do you think we will ever see our father again?" Robin asked longingly.

Sarah didn't know the answer, but she did know one thing. "You have two Bill Marshes trying to find a way to get you home. I think your odds are pretty good!"

"Never thought of it that way," Robin said, and both girls visibly cheered up.

"It's weird," Diane said. "You *are* Grandma. Except for the memories and being able to say, 'Remember this' or 'Remember that,' you are exactly the same person. Grandpa too."

"We can tell how you will react to something, what you will say or do," continued Robin. "But Uncle Bill is different."

"Yeah," Diane said. "He's…" She couldn't find the right word. "He's…stiffer, grouchier. Kind of like Dad on a bad day when he's running out of patience."

Being a mother, Sarah understood exactly what the girls were saying. It was precisely those memories Diane had mentioned that made the difference between the two Bill Marshes. Their Bill Marsh had raised two daughters. He remembered all of the "firsts"—first teeth, first steps, first words. He remembered the falls and the triumphs, the laughter and the tears, the praises and the scoldings, the arms around his neck, and the kisses on his cheeks. He'd seen their eyes bright with wonder when he showed them something new, and he had wiped the tears from those same eyes when they were scared or hurt. All of the things that, over the years, had smoothed his rough edges.

Her Bill Marsh still had his rough edges, and Sarah wondered how he would deal with these girls in the weeks to come.

Marsh couldn't stop the thought from echoing in his mind…"What if…"

He sat down on the porch steps and looked up at the night sky, the same sky he used to gaze at as a boy as he dreamed of being a starship captain.

The screen door opened behind him and, for a second, the darkness lit up as the light from the house escaped. And then, as the door closed, it became dark once again. Marsh heard his mother's steps and automatically slid over to make room for her. She sat down quietly, respecting the silence of the night and her son's thoughts. He looked over and smiled at her, a warm smile that expressed his appreciation for her company, and then he went back to his scrutiny of the heavens. They sat that way for a while, mother and son, both thinking of the young girls sleeping upstairs.

"What's the matter, Bill?" his mother asked, her voice so soft it blended with the black velvet night. Sarah knew what the galaxy thought of her son, what it expected of him, and she knew that he could deliver whatever was needed. But none of that mattered to her. When she looked at him, she only saw her child. And tonight she knew her child was troubled.

Marsh shrugged and shook his head, frustrated, not sure how to respond. His mind was still a jumble of thoughts and unfamiliar emotions.

She understood, though, and chuckled to herself. "It's okay, Bill," she said quietly and patted his knee. "Children can do that to you." Then she went back inside and left him alone with the stars…and his thoughts.

The girls were in the barn, bidding farewell to their horses. Gerroll was checking the shuttlecraft for departure, and Marsh was in the kitchen saying goodbye to his parents.

"I'm so glad you came," his mother said. "Not just because of the girls, but because it's nice to have you home."

"I'm glad I came too, Mom. I wish I could do it more often."

"We do too," his father agreed, "but we're proud of you and what you do."

They both hugged him and he returned their hugs, wondering when he'd be able to do it again.

"Your father and I have made a decision about something and we need to tell you."

The tone of her voice indicated that she was going to tell him something serious, and he regarded her intently. "What is it, Mom?" he asked as he leaned against the counter, knowing better than to jump up and sit on it—she always scolded him when he did. It was a funny thought, and he smiled to himself—he was a starship commander and yet he was worried that his mother would reprimand him. It was true—no matter how old you got or what your responsibilities in the real world were, when you were in your parents' home, you were still a child.

"If you can't get the girls back home…"

"We will, Mom. Don't worry," he assured her, although he really wasn't so sure just how he was going to manage that feat.

"But if you can't, we want you to bring them back here," she declared.

"Here? Are you sure?"

"Yes, Bill, here!" his father said adamantly. "Your mother and I will raise them."

Marsh didn't know why he was so surprised, but he was. He stared out the kitchen window and watched the horses in the corral while he thought about what his parents wanted to do. "That's a big responsibility, Dad."

"What will you do with them?" his mother asked, obviously annoyed with him. "Give them to strangers? Leave them in an orphanage on some strange planet? Raise them yourself?"

"You know I can't do that."

"Then what, Bill?" She was demanding an answer, and he didn't have one.

"I don't know, Mom," he said. "To be honest, I haven't thought about it. My goal is to get them back where they belong."

"And if you can't? Then they belong here with us," his father said, leaving very little room for discussion.

Marsh sighed. They were right, and he slowly nodded his head. "Okay. If we can't get them home—but I plan to do just that—I'll bring them back here to live. I promise."

"Thank you, Bill," his mother said, sounding relieved. "Although I hope you can get them home, for their sake."

She looked at him and smiled, her eyes suddenly alive and dancing. "If you do, will you bring them yourself? Will you meet…their father?" she questioned, clearly amused by the thought.

Marsh never got that far in his thinking, and he looked at her with wide-eyed amazement. "I…I don't…know," he said, trying to imagine the scenario.

"Well, if you do, please tell him something for me."

"Sure. What?" This was one hell of a bizarre conversation.

"Tell him he did a great job raising them."

"Okay." He didn't know what else to say.

Her face turned serious again and she gently touched his arm. "Take care of them," she said.

"I will."

"And Bill?"

"What, Mom?"

"Let your guard down. They're young girls. *Be* their uncle. They need you. Remember, in another universe you are their father, and they have proved that you are capable of being a great one. Use that knowledge to help them."

"I'll try," Marsh promised, but wondered if he really could.

They were standing in the field next to the shuttlecraft. It was hard for the girls to say goodbye to the elder Marshes. They had made them feel welcome and at home, so much like their real grandparents. In this new universe, they were the ones that made each day easier to get through.

"Will we see you again?" Robin asked them, but looked at Uncle Bill for the answer.

Marsh didn't know how to respond—these girls had a habit of putting him in that predicament, and he didn't like it. He didn't want to tell them that this is where they'd be living if he couldn't get them home. No one was ready to think of that possibility. So, he gave them the only answer he could think of…"We'll see." He smiled and shook his head as soon as he said it, realizing he had just given the quintessential parental answer. He was learning fast.

"If we don't see you before we leave, maybe we could come back and visit," Diane suggested, and then added, "After we go home, that is." She and Robin had already thought about this.

"Yeah," Robin said. "If we got here once, we could probably do it again!"

Oh, no, Marsh thought, they were already planning to come back. *They're kidding, right?*

"As our Gerroll always says," Diane quoted, "'Anything can happen and the fun is in the trying.'"

Marsh grinned and looked at Gerroll, who nodded his approval, shrugged, and said, "Can't argue with brilliance."

The newly found granddaughters and grandparents hugged each other tightly and said goodbye, each pair wondering what the future held.

CHAPTER 18

A New Polaris

The day-long journey back to the Polaris was a little tedious for them all, especially the girls. The shuttlecraft was small and there wasn't much room to maneuver. Marsh and Gerroll were used to it—they'd been confined for longer periods. At the Academy, training missions on shuttlecrafts sometimes lasted for weeks at a time. The girls, however, were uncomfortable.

Marsh used the time to try to piece together the missing details he hadn't been able to get from the girls in New Mexico, especially about their time on the alien ship, which they had wanted to forget. He wasn't sure whether they were beginning to open up to him or they were just so bored they'd talk about anything, but they finally told him about their adventure.

He was impressed with their tale. They'd been frightened and unsure, but had kept their composure, pooled their resources, and done what they had to do to survive. They really were quite a little duo.

Unfortunately, they talked incessantly. Mostly to each other, about everything and anything, and Marsh wondered how they could possibly find so much to say. The girls had moved to the back of the shuttle, but it was a small ship, and he couldn't help but hear the constant chatter and giggles. Images of muzzles danced in his head.

"Are they driving you crazy as well, Gerroll?" Marsh whispered to his second-in-command.

No response.

Marsh leaned closer and asked again, but still got no response.

"GERROLL?" Marsh asked in the loudest whisper he could manage.

"Yes, Captain?" Gerroll inquired casually. "Were you saying something?"

"Yes, Gerroll. I wanted to know if their chatter is driving you crazy."

"No, Sir."

"It's not?" Marsh couldn't believe it.

"No. I blocked it out hours ago."

"Blocked it out? How?" Marsh asked, desperate for the solution.

"Nimians have powers of concentration that humans do not. We need it in order to block out constantly reading other people's thoughts. I just focus my mind elsewhere and I do not hear anything else."

"Nothing?"

"Nothing."

"Can you teach me, Gerroll? Now?"

"No, Bill. It takes years of training."

Resigned, Marsh sighed deeply. "This is going to be a very long trip!" He leaned back in his chair, closed his eyes, and dreamed about the quiet of his quarters.

When they arrived back on the Polaris, it was late in the day and Marsh had a lot to do. First things first… he had to get Diane and Robin settled so he could go about his business. After dropping off his things, they stood outside his quarters while he wondered where to put them.

"Which quarters do you occupy on *your* Polaris?" he inquired, although he doubted they would be able to have the same ones on his ship.

"The ones next to yours," Robin told him and pointed to the door only a few feet from his. Her tone suggested that there couldn't possibly be any other choice.

Interesting, Marsh thought. The quarters next to his was always kept empty to insure his privacy…and the walls *were* soundproof! Besides, he wanted to keep a close eye on them anyway. *Why not?*

"Okay," he said, nodding. "That can be arranged here too." He turned to Gerroll. "I've asked Lieutenant Diska to meet us here. I think she's a good choice to help get the girls settled. They've mentioned that they know her well on their Polaris. I will meet you on the bridge shortly."

"Yes, Captain," Gerroll said. He winked at Diane and Robin, then turned and headed for the hyperlift. The doors slid open just as he approached. Lieutenant Helen Diska stepped out.

"Lieutenant," Marsh said, calling her over, "I'd like you to meet Diane and Robin. They are...uh..." Marsh hadn't yet decided on how much to tell his crew, so for now he settled on, "They will be staying with us for a while."

Lieutenant Diska smiled a very welcoming smile at the sisters, and the girls knew at once that she was just like their own Helen Diska, whom they were very close to. Plus, being the communications officer, Lieutenant Diska always knew all of the ship's good gossip and would sometimes let something slip. It was also thanks to her that Diane and Robin got away with so many pranks. It was her job to monitor communications, and she never told their father if she heard they were up to something they shouldn't be. She never lied for them if he asked, which was fair, but she never volunteered information, either. Lieutenant Diska was also the one who tipped them off when their father found them out, so they could be prepared for his visit.

To the girls, Marsh said, "I know you don't have much in the way of luggage. I'm sure that between the ship's stores and the replicators we can get you everything you need. I have assigned Lieutenant Diska to help you get settled. Let her know what you want and she will see that you get it. I will have the automated food dispenser turned on in your quarters in case you are hungry. I have a lot to do on the bridge. It's been a long day for both of you and I suggest you go to sleep as soon as you're settled in. I will see you in the morning. We will have breakfast together and then we need to talk."

Marsh informed Diska which quarters he had assigned the girls, then started to turn toward the hyperlift. He was stopped by Diane calling him.

"Uncle Bill?"

Lieutenant Diska's mouth opened in surprise when she heard Marsh being called "uncle." He looked at her, shrugged slightly, but didn't respond verbally to the question her eyes were asking. His demeanor let her know that he would explain later.

"What?" Marsh asked impatiently.

"Will you come say good night?" Diane inquired timidly. Both girls had caught his tone and they waited nervously for his reply.

While they had been in New Mexico, his mother had gone in every evening to chat with the girls before they went to sleep. He had only yelled a quick "good night" as they were on their way up the stairs. It hadn't occurred to him that it would be *his* job now to make sure that they were settled in for the night. But he also knew that, except for him, they were alone.

"Well, okay. I'll stop in before my last shift on the bridge," he told them.

The girls smiled at each other. That's when their father stopped in every night also.

"You'll tuck us in?" Robin asked, smiling playfully.

"Yeah, sure." He couldn't even look at Helen Diska now. He didn't want to see the look that was probably spread across her entire face. He wondered what the girls would tell her before he got a chance to explain.

"I'll take care of everything, Captain," Helen assured him quickly. She was eager for him to go back to the bridge so she could find out what was going on.

The girls noticed his uneasiness and took advantage of it.

"Bye, *Uncle Bill*," Diane said, deliberately accenting his name. She gave him a small wave and an innocent smile.

"Have fun on the bridge, *Uncle Bill*. We'll see you later," Robin added, and smiled as angelically as her sister.

He nodded, uncertain of what else to do, and entered the hyperlift, but not before he turned and gave his two charges a warning look. They waved and brightened their smiles. As the doors closed, he heard them burst into laughter. *Surely not a good sign,* he thought.

"Don't keep me in suspense," Helen said immediately upon his departure. "'Uncle Bill?' You called him 'Uncle Bill.' I didn't know he had nieces," she admitted, and waited impatiently for the girls to explain.

"Well," Diane said seriously, "we didn't want to call him 'Daddy.' I'm sure you would agree. You know, under the circumstances."

Helen Diska stopped dead in her tracks and stared at both girls. She ran her fingers through her thick, dark hair, combing her bangs out of her eyes, as if that would help her to see the situation more clearly. She'd known Bill Marsh for at least twelve years and thought she knew everything there was to know about him. "'Daddy?' Did you say 'Daddy?'" she asked, certain she couldn't possibly have heard correctly.

"Yes," Robin said, beginning to giggle. "But we felt uncomfortable calling him that." Unlike her sister, she was having a hard time keeping a straight face.

"I…I don't…um…understand," Helen stammered, her gray eyes concentrating on the two girls in front of her. Now that she looked at them, she realized there was a family resemblance…vague, but there, nonetheless.

"You don't?" Diane questioned. "You mean he didn't tell you…about us?"

Helen numbly shook her head. She didn't know what to say.

"Then I guess we'll have to tell you," Robin said, laughing.

"Come on," Diane said, and led the stunned communications officer into the quarters they had been assigned. "Have we got a story for you!"

"We *are* going to tell her the truth, aren't we?" Robin whispered as she passed her sister.

Diane hesitated and grinned. "Yeah, we'd better unless we want to spend the night in the brig!"

"And the rest of our lives in our quarters!" Robin added.

CHAPTER 19

LET YOUR GUARD DOWN

It felt good to be back on the bridge, in comfortable territory. Marsh settled into his command chair and began to get caught up on the past week's activities. He spoke with Matt Wells and explained what had transpired over the past few days. Luckily, the doctor was tying up loose ends and would be finished on Saras in the morning. Perfect timing. Then they could move on. Just where, Marsh wasn't sure. He and Gerroll had been discussing numerous theories and possibilities, but as of yet, they hadn't come up with a course of action to get the girls back home. When he finished on the bridge, he headed to engineering to see Kate Wells, who was repairing a circuit panel that had overloaded earlier in the day.

"It's good to see you, Bill," Kate said, smiling broadly when he entered her engineering room.

"It's good to be back, Kate. How are the repairs coming?"

"I should be done soon. Minor damage. Nothing to worry about." She pushed some loose strands of hair off her face and turned back to the circuit panel.

"Can I help?" He had a lot of pent-up energy and wouldn't mind doing something that would take his mind off his other problems.

"That would be great. Between the two of us we could be done in a couple of hours."

Kate showed Marsh the burnt circuit panel and they got to work. It felt good to be doing something constructive, and he told Kate about the events of the last week while they worked. She listened, flabbergasted, not only at the story, but also at the fact that Bill Marsh now had two young girls in his care. She'd known him since their first year at the Academy, and there was no way she could even begin to imagine him with children. He was not a man of great patience when kids were concerned. He barely interacted with any of the children on the ship, except to lay down the law if they became unruly. He was pleasant enough to Jared, but Kate assumed that was only because Jared was her and Matt's son, and because Marsh had known Jared since he was born. Jared, however, like all the other kids, stayed out of Marsh's way.

"What do you think, Kate?"

"It's almost fixed, Bill."

"No, not about the circuit panel, Kate. About the girls."

She chose her words carefully. "Well, Bill, raising children can be challenging."

"I have no intention of raising them, Kate. I plan to get them home as soon as possible."

"I know. But until you do, you are their acting guardian."

Sighing heavily, he admitted reluctantly, "I'm not father material, Kate. I'm having a rough time with this whole thing."

Glad that he at least recognized his shortcomings, Kate answered, "I'm sure you are. It isn't easy, that's for sure. Matt and I will help in any way we can, you know that, but, from what you've told me, the girls have a very strong bond with their father. It's you they will turn to."

Marsh leaned against the wall and looked at his head engineer, who luckily was also his good friend. "I don't know what to do, Kate." It was hard for him to admit, even to himself, that these two young girls could have him feeling so baffled and unsure.

Kate smiled. "Let your guard down, Bill."

Marsh laughed. "My mother told me the exact same thing."

"Well, then maybe you should listen."

"I'm working on it, Katie. I'm working on it."

It took Marsh longer in engineering than he expected and, by the time he got to the girls' quarters, it was late. When he entered, they were in bed with the lights out.

He walked quietly over to the first bed and saw

that Diane was already asleep. Her hair was tangled and damp, and he could see she had been crying. *Was she upset because I didn't show up to say good night*, he wondered, *or was she just homesick*? He resisted the urge to brush the tears from her still-wet cheeks. He didn't know if sleep had come easily and didn't want to wake her, so he gently fixed her covers instead and moved to the other sleeping child a few feet away.

Robin was not awake, but not asleep either, lingering in the stage that danced between real thoughts and dreams. She opened her eyes and then closed them, not really focusing, and groggily said, "Good night, Daddy," as she turned on her side.

The words startled him. He had barely gotten used to the girls calling him "Uncle Bill," but he only hesitated a second before whispering in a voice so tender that it surprised even himself, "Good night, Robin." Then he fixed her covers also, and left the room.

In the light of the corridor, he took a deep breath, straightened his tunic, and headed back to the bridge, his whole being slightly off kilter.

CHAPTER 20

ZURALITE CRYSTALS

Marsh still had a lot to catch up on, so he and the girls ate a fast breakfast in his office. He only had a cup of coffee, black and strong. The girls sat across from him and used his desk as a table while they munched on peanut butter and jelly sandwiches.

He scrunched his nose at the smell of the peanut butter. They laughed at that, and he said, "I don't care for it."

"Dad doesn't, either," Robin said. "He teases us about our infatuation with it."

"You said last night that you wanted to talk to us. Have you found a way to get us home?" Diane asked anxiously. She was folding her napkin into tiny little squares and then watching it unfold as she let it go.

"No, not yet, but we're working on it. We will find a way. Don't worry. You might be here for a while, though, and that's why I wanted to talk to you."

He didn't waste any time. There was something he needed to clarify immediately, before he got on with his day. "I suppose you have rules on your Polaris."

"*Rules?*" Diane asked, as if she'd never heard the word and needed a dictionary to define it.

"Yes, you know, the things you can and cannot do," he prompted her.

"Yeah, a few," she answered, and both girls laughed.

Concluding that meant there were a lot of rules, Marsh held out his hand to indicate she should continue. "For instance…"

"Well, let's see…" Robin said, "School is optional and we have full run of the ship!" She popped the last of her sandwich in her mouth and smiled at him.

"Hmmm. Funny, but I thought your father would think more like me on this one." He returned her smile. "Would you like to try again?"

The girls sighed and then went back and forth reciting their father's strict orders.

"Okay," Diane started, "we're not allowed on the bridge unless we ask permission and Dad says it's okay."

"We're not allowed in engineering at all," Robin stated.

"Actually," Diane added, rolling her eyes, "we're not allowed *anywhere* that interferes with the running of the ship."

Robin thought for a second and then said, "We're not allowed in the main rec room after 1900 hours."

"We have to report to the sickbay during a Priority

1 alert because Dad says it's the safest part of the ship," Diane told him.

"Okay." Marsh put up his hand to stop the recitation. He knew they were well-versed, and their father had taught them well. "Same rules apply here. Understand?"

Two bobbing heads.

He remembered his mother and Kate's advice. The words "let your guard down" kept playing in his head. He tried to be more amiable. "All of the ship's recreational facilities are open to you. You can use any of them, but let me know where you are at all times. And I mean...*at all times*." Relax, he reminded himself again. "Are there any places in particular you like to go?" he asked, trying to soften his tone.

"The geology lab," Robin said. "Dad lets me. I don't get in the way. Honest."

"You like geology?" *Interesting hobby for a young girl*, he thought.

"Yes, at home I have a great collection of rocks and minerals. Dad takes us down to as many planets as he can, and I collect them."

"Okay. I can arrange for you to visit the lab. Diane, where do you like to go?"

"My favorite place is the arboretum. I like to sit there and read."

"That would be fine. It's one of my favorite places too." Marsh looked at them both. "I have arranged for you to attend classes here, same as if you were home. When you leave my office, see Lieutenant Carin. She's expecting you. And girls, I expect you to behave."

"We will," they said together.

"All right. I'll see you later," he said, not really sure whether to believe them or not.

On the way out Robin noticed a crystal sitting on the shelf behind his desk. "Uncle Bill, is that a Zuralite crystal?" she asked as she pointed to the small, milky-white stone.

"You know what it is?" he asked, impressed with her knowledge. "A crewman gave it to me. He picked it up on one of the planets we were surveying." Marsh picked up the crystal and showed it to her. "Would you like to have it?" he asked.

Robin looked at her sister and then back at him. "No, thanks. I'd better not."

It looked exactly like the best of the four Zuralite crystals she had once picked up...

Robin thought her father would say that it would be okay. She'd been counting on it. It never dawned on her that he would refuse her request.

"Why not?" she asked angrily.

"Because it's too dangerous," Marsh replied.

"It is not! You're just saying that! I'm going anyway!" she screamed at him. How, she didn't know, but she was going to go no matter what he said. She started to get up.

"Sit down, Robin," Marsh commanded.

"No!" she said and continued her ascent.

She stood up.

He stood up.

She sat down. But not happily.

Marsh remained standing, came around to the front of his desk and sat down on the edge of it, directly in front of his daughter. "Now listen to me, Robin. The planet is unstable. Earthquakes occur at any time. This is not the only planet that has Zuralite crystals, and you will have to wait until we find a more suitable planet for you to search for them."

Robin continued her argument. "But you sent exploration teams down. A few of them. Why can't I go with one of them?"

"I already explained why. Besides, the exploration teams have work to do. It is not the time or the place for you to be there. That's all there is to it."

"May I ask the team that hasn't gone down yet to try and find me some crystals?" She'd rather do it herself, it was more fun, but at least she'd get the crystals to add to her rapidly growing collection of rocks and minerals.

"Sorry, Robin. They need to work as quickly as possible while they still have time. I don't want them distracted."

She sat and glared at him, knowing it would be no use to try to change his mind. "May I go now?" she asked curtly, tears of frustration and disappointment stinging her eyes.

"Yes, you may." He would not allow her tears to alter his decision.

Robin stormed out his office and headed for her quarters. Suddenly, she understood her sister's affinity for slamming doors and the frustration it must release. She would have loved to slam one in his face! She'd find Diane and vent. At least there was someone who understood, even if her father didn't.

On the way to her quarters, she passed the transporter room. She hesitated. What would be the big deal if she asked one of the crewmembers to look for crystals for her? They wouldn't have to go into the caves. Maybe there would be some lying around. Highly unlikely, considering the crystals formed in dark caves, but you never know, maybe she'd get lucky. Of course, if they did find her one, she'd have to keep it hidden—not an easy feat with a Zuralite crystal—and she'd never be able to show it to her father.

She would see who was waiting to transport down. If it were someone she knew and could trust, then she would ask them to do it. Much to her surprise, the room was empty. No more exploration teams? *she wondered to herself.* Not fair! I want those crystals.

The lure of the transporter was too much. It was probably still set with the right coordinates for the planet's surface. Jared had taught her and Diane how to do a simple transport, but if their parents ever found out they would probably be grounded for life. Not thinking twice, she set the dials and jumped on the transporter platform. She knew the planet had a breathable atmosphere and that she wouldn't need a spacesuit. Her only problem was how to get back to the ship, but she'd worry about that later. If Lieutenant Diska would connect her to Diane without her father knowing, then Diane could sneak down to the transporter room and get her back up.

When she materialized, she was on the planet's surface. Perfect! *she thought. A fast look around the area didn't show any crewmembers.* They must be farther away taking readings and collecting samples.

Robin started looking for the nearest cave. The faster she could get out of sight, the better.

"Gerroll, have all the exploration teams returned to the ship?" Marsh asked.

"Yes, Captain. The last team returned a few minutes ago."

"Good. Let's prepare to leave orbit. Ensign Walker," Marsh called to his navigator, "plot a course for the Maderan colony. We have medical supplies to deliver."

"Course plotted and programmed, Sir."

"Take us out." Marsh commanded. The stars streaked by, and the viewscreen glowed with a white light as the Polaris slipped into accelerated hyperspeed.

It certainly is an ugly planet, *Robin thought as she looked around. It's amazing that such beautiful crystals could be found here, assuming, that is, if she found some. The ground rumbled continuously, and it gave her a very unsteady feeling. Hopefully, she'd be safely back aboard before any major earthquakes struck.*

She didn't have to go far to find a cave. Standing at the entrance, she gave a quick prayer that it would be safe. She took a few steps inside. It was very unsettling being inside a cave while the ground shook underneath. She'd have to make this real fast. Quickly, she ventured to the back of the cave and knew instantly she had hit pay dirt. She could see the crystals glowing from where she stood, giving the whole cave an eerie radiance. She took a few more steps and had her pick of the most beautiful crystals she'd ever seen.

Zuralite crystals glow continuously, casting a rainbow of colors in all directions. In the light they looked rather ordinary. It wasn't until you saw them in the dark, their natural habitat, that their true, awesome beauty was revealed.

Robin chose her crystals carefully, turning them over and over, inspecting them for any tiny flaw. They weren't big and she took four of the best—three for her and one for Diane. She tucked them carefully in her pockets for safekeeping and then ran out of the cave as fast as she could.

As soon as she was out, she tapped her communication badge and hailed Lieutenant Diska. At least she tried to. There wasn't any response. She tried again and again. Nothing but static. Maybe I can find some members of the exploration team, *she thought, and she went in search of somebody…anybody.*

It was getting late and getting dark, and by the time Robin realized she was all alone on the desolate planet, she was getting very, very scared.

Diane looked all over the ship for her sister, but couldn't find her, so she went to lunch alone.

"Where's your sister?" Marsh asked.

She hesitated before answering, not wanting to get her sister into any trouble, but she really didn't know where Robin was and she was getting nervous. "I don't know."

"Are you sure?"

"Yes. I haven't seen her since this morning."

"What time?"

"I don't know, Dad…since breakfast."

Marsh knew that he had seen Robin after breakfast when she requested permission to transport down with one of the exploration teams. She had left his office angry and upset. He didn't like the thought that was nagging in the back of his mind. "I'm going back to the bridge. Finish your lunch. I'll see you later."

Suddenly, Diane wasn't hungry. After her father left, she went back to her quarters to wait for her sister.

"Gerroll, check the transporter logs. Do the records show everyone accounted for?" Marsh asked.

"One moment, Captain, I will check."

Marsh waited impatiently while Gerroll did the research, but he knew the answer before Gerroll confirmed it.

"No, Captain, the logs don't match. There is one transport down with no return."

"Well, Gerroll, it seems that Robin snuck down after everyone transported back, and that is where she still is. Ensign Walker, plot a course back to the planet and get there as fast as you can."

"Yes, Captain. Course plotted and programmed."

"How long will it take us?"

"One hour, ten minutes."

Marsh paced the entire time.

It was getting cold, but Robin was afraid to go back into the cave. The rumbling was getting stronger, and she knew it was safer to stay out in the open in case of a full-fledged earthquake. She huddled under some trees where she could move quickly. She knew her father would figure out where she was—it was just a matter of time—but she didn't know how much time she had. Without warning, a gigantic boulder, loosened by the shaking ground, came tumbling and roaring down the hillside next to her, followed by large rocks and debris. She ran out of harm's way but tripped and fell. A huge fault line opened next to her and she had to scramble to keep from falling into the abyss. As she tried to scurry to safety, she saw a figure materialize a few feet from her.

Marsh ran to her, helped her to her feet, and held her tightly. She was shaking like a leaf in his arms. He hailed the ship. "Kate, two to transport up. Hurry…we're in the midst of an earthquake!"

"Where have you been?" Diane yelled and rushed to meet Robin as soon as her sister walked into their quarters.

Robin didn't answer, but instead took the carefully concealed crystals from her pockets and dimmed the lights.

"Oh, wow! Those crystals are magnificent," Diane said in amazement. "Look at the rainbows all over the walls."

With the lights back on, Robin found them a safe hiding place.

"I'm almost afraid to ask, Rob. What did Dad say?"

Robin grimaced. "You know what he said…'Go to your quarters. I'll be there shortly,'" she mimicked. "He was real angry, so hopefully it will take him a while to cool down and get here."

They talked while Robin changed her clothes and told her sister about her adventure. Unfortunately, he showed up sooner rather than later.

"Diane, give us a few minutes alone, please," Marsh said when he walked in.

Diane gave Robin a reassuring smile on her way out, but knew it wouldn't help much.

Marsh stood directly in front of his daughter and got right to the point. "You caused us all a lot of worry today."

"I'm sorry."

He nodded at her, not doubting her remorse. "I want you to pack up your entire collection of rocks and minerals. I'll wait while you do it."

"Why?" she asked, alarmed.

"I think you know why, Robin. There are consequences for your actions today. I'll be taking them away from you for awhile. I have carts outside to take them to the cargo bay." Knowing how extensive and heavy her collection was, he brought three anti-gravity carriers that could float through the corridors and bring the rocks to the storage area.

"How long?" she asked, dreading his answer. Working with her rocks was her favorite pastime, and she spent hours cataloging and researching her growing collection.

"One month."

"No, you can't do that!" she cried, no longer contrite. Her arms were crossed in determination and tears were brimming in the corners of her eyes. "It's not fair!" she yelled in defiance.

He did his best to remain calm. "Not fair? Really? Answer me this…how do you think I felt when I realized what you had done? Not only was I angry that you disobeyed me, but I had to turn this ship around to get you—on top of being worried sick the entire time that *something might have happened to you." He didn't give her a chance to answer. "Now, pack up your rocks. You're losing them for a month. And, you're confined to your quarters for two weeks."*

Feet dragging, Robin did as she was told, silently saying goodbye to each precious stone as she packed it inside one of the specially built carrying cases he had made for her.

When she finished, Marsh dimmed the lights. In the semi-darkness, he looked around and quickly spotted what he had been searching for. No amount of hiding could dim the bright glow of Zuralite crystals. He took them from under a throw pillow on the couch where she thought she had hidden them so well.

"What are you going to do with them?" she asked apprehensively.

"Transport them back down to the planet's surface."

"No! Daddy, please don't!"

"Sorry Robin, you can't keep treasures you got through disobeying." And treasures they were. Even he was impressed by their luminescence.

Marsh left her, rockless for a month, and headed for the transporter room. But not before he took the best crystal and popped it into his pocket. He'd save it for the future and give it to her on a worthy occasion.

The girls left Marsh's office and headed for the hyperlift.

"I can't believe we have to go to class," Robin said and pouted.

"Yeah. Under the circumstances, you'd think he'd let us have some time off," Diane agreed. "Deck 12," she instructed the hyperlift as they entered. "I'll bet you Dad wouldn't make us go," she said, although they both knew that he would.

The girls leaned against the wall and waited silently until they reached their destination.

"We could go to the Simulation Deck instead," Robin suggested as the door slid open. "Our programs won't be there, but maybe the other kids programmed some good adventures."

On their Polaris, the girls spent as much time as they were allowed in one of the five Simulation Decks. There, they could instruct the computer to provide any kind of environment they wanted. Robin had caves programmed where she could go digging for rocks and minerals. Diane went horseback riding on simulated horses that were so real, she had to remind herself that they weren't. Both girls had visited planets from all over the galaxy without ever leaving the ship. They became characters in books they loved or made up their own stories, with adventures as exotic as their imaginations could make them. Plus, there were preprogrammed scenarios that taught lessons by allowing the student to be an interactive part of the instruction. Sometimes, classes were held on the Sim Deck and the whole class participated as they journeyed back through time or traveled to distant planets for history or geography lessons. Their father limited the time they were allowed to spend on the Simulation Deck, and it was one of the first privileges he took away when they misbehaved.

"Maybe we better go to class first," Diane said. "If

Uncle Bill is anything like Dad and we don't show up for class…"

"Yeah, I know," Robin finished the thought, "we won't be allowed on the Sim Deck at all. Okay, school first."

Lieutenant Carin was waiting for them and stopped the class as soon as Diane and Robin entered. The girls looked around and were shocked that they knew every single face. On their Polaris, these kids were their friends, but here, the faces stared blankly back at them. Diane and Robin walked tentatively to the front of the room. It felt strange to be so nervous in an environment that was usually so familiar and friendly.

Sensing the girls' discomfort, Lieutenant Carin smiled warmly at them. "Hello, girls," she said and ushered the two sisters to stand on either side of her. "I have already explained to the class why you are here. Captain Marsh said it would be all right. It is absolutely incredible that you are from a parallel universe! I hope you'll tell us all about your Polaris."

"Yeah, and how you manage to get along with Captain Marsh!" came a voice from the back of the room.

"Well, Jared," Diane said smiling, "on our Polaris even *you* get along with him!"

"You know me?" Jared asked loudly so he could be heard above everyone's snickering.

"Of course we know you! We grew up together. Don't your grandparents have a ranch next to the Marshes' ranch?" Robin asked.

"Yes," Jared answered, still puzzled. "So what?"

"In our universe, Robin and I were raised on the ranch until we were five years old and we go back every summer with you—or rather your counterpart—to visit. We've known our Jared forever! He's our best friend," Diane explained.

"Wow!" Jared exclaimed. "I have a counterpart! That's amazing! I never thought about it. So, you really do know me…I mean, my counterpart."

"Yes," Robin said. "We know *all* of you!"

There were only twelve kids in their class and, to prove their point, the sisters went around the room naming each one. The class was suddenly a beehive of shocked chatter and activity, everyone asking questions about their counterparts in the parallel universe.

Diane and Robin were laughing. "And, believe it or not," Robin said when the room finally quieted, "Dad gets along with all of the kids. He even comes in once a month to teach a class on space exploration! Everyone loves it!"

"Except for his assignments!" Diane added, and everyone groaned in understanding.

No one could believe that the strict, stone-faced Captain Marsh would actually come in to teach a class…and that it would be fun.

"Why don't you ask him?" Diane suggested. "He's really okay. Honest."

A sea of dubious faces met her recommendation, and she had to admit that, knowing her father's counterpart, she understood their doubt. "Well, give him some time. He's coming around." The class continued to stare at her as if she was crazy. She rethought the suggestion and muttered, "Sort of."

The sisters began to feel comfortable in this room of strangers who weren't really strangers after all.

"We were just about to start a history lesson. What are you learning in your class," Lieutenant Carin queried.

"World War III on Earth," Robin answered, already bored with the idea of sitting through a history lecture.

"That's what we're up to also!" Lieutenant Carin stated enthusiastically. "Take a seat and join the class. We'll do some preliminary work here and then we'll go to the Simulation Deck and witness some of the pivotal battles. Then we can all take roles and become part of the peace negotiations."

"I'd rather go horseback riding," Diane whispered to Robin as she remembered the fabulous Nimian horse Gerroll had programmed for her.

"Or cave mining," Robin whispered back.

But they took their seats, same as the ones on their Polaris, and tried to pay attention.

It was getting harder and harder to tell the universes apart!

CHAPTER 21

A SARAS FAIRY

Marsh had just heard from Lieutenant Carin and was glad to hear that the girls were doing well. No sooner had he broken his connection with her, he was contacted by Matt Wells, who was still on Saras. "Bill, I think you'd better transport down right away."

He's definitely excited about something, Marsh thought. "What's up, Matt?"

"I was telling Ambassador Kaner about Diane and Robin, and he thinks he might have a theory. I think you should hear it for yourself."

Marsh looked at Gerroll who was smiling and nodding his head. "We're on our way!"

Saras had the most beautiful sky Marsh had ever seen. It was blue, similar to Earth's, but a deeper, richer shade. The clouds, however, were an iridescent pink that glowed as if illuminated from behind, and the edges looked as if they were outlined in silver. It made him think of an enchanted city and he expected to see little fairies flying around. Maybe, with some luck, one of those imaginary fairies would land on his shoulder and whisper the answer to his problem.

Two city officials greeted them and immediately took Marsh and Gerroll to Ambassador Kaner's chambers, where Matt Wells was also waiting. Marsh had met Kaner when the Polaris first arrived. After that, it had been Matt's project, and Marsh hadn't been involved, except for authorizing supply transports and computer use, all of which he automatically agreed to.

"It's nice to see you again, Captain," Kaner said and shook his hand. "Your doctor has been an invaluable help to us. We're sorry to see him go."

"Yes, Ambassador, we like him too," Marsh replied, smiling at his friend. "Dr. Wells says you have a theory about our young visitors. I'd like to hear it, Sir."

"By all means, Captain. Please come and sit down." He led them to a soft, circular gray couch, which was positioned in front of a huge picture window.

Marsh, Gerroll, and Wells took seats and waited expectantly to hear what Kaner had to tell them.

"Can I offer you some refreshment, Captain?" Kaner inquired.

"No thank you, Ambassador," Marsh said, responding for all his men. He was getting antsy. He just wanted answers.

"Then let me begin," Kaner said, and Marsh leaned forward to give the ambassador his full attention.

"I don't know if you are aware of this, but our planet has numerous outposts—research colonies mostly—further out in space, not far from the Frazon boundary."

"No, I was not aware of that," Marsh said, then looked at Gerroll who was also shaking his head.

The ambassador continued. "A few months ago, these outposts were plagued by four instances of kidnapping…infants, actually."

Marsh was astonished. "Kidnapping? That's almost unheard of these days."

"Yes, well, almost, but not completely. There was a fifth attempt, but the outposts were on high alert and one of the kidnappers was captured, but not before being fatally wounded. He was brought to the hospital, although there was nothing we could do to save him. But before he died, the doctor gave him an injection filled with some kind of truth serum to make him talk, and he told quite a bizarre story. We never knew if it was the truth or a hypnotic-hallucinogenic side effect."

"That's a possibility, Captain," Wells said. "Sometimes these new drugs have an adverse effect."

"What did he tell you, Ambassador?" Gerroll asked.

"He claimed he was a crew member on a Mog ship—"

"Mog?" Marsh interrupted. "What is a Mog?"

"According to our prisoner, the Mog are a race of people who are governed by the Frazons."

"The Frazons," Marsh muttered and shook his head. They were the last people he wanted to tangle with.

Kaner went on. "This Mog vessel is a renegade ship, led by an ex-military commander who finds it more profitable to kidnap and sell children than to be in the military."

"Pleasant fellow," Wells said, and shuddered as he thought of his own son.

Marsh nodded his head in agreement, but knew that kidnapping would verify the girls' story.

"Here's the interesting part," Kaner continued, "the part we could never decide if it were true or not. Supposedly, this commander accidentally found a portal in Frazon space that led to a parallel universe…"

Now it's beginning to fit, Marsh thought excitedly. He looked at Gerroll who was listening carefully with a glint of anticipation in his eyes.

"…and he brings children back and forth through this portal. Kidnapping them on one side and selling them on the other."

"Making them untraceable," Marsh reasoned aloud. He shook his head in disbelief.

"Yes," Kaner said, "but there's more."

"More?" Marsh asked in amazement. *How much worse can it get?*

"Yes. Our captive told us that the commander has a very unique way of picking his crew members, as well as the children he kidnaps."

"And that is?" Gerroll asked.

"This is what we were told: With the use of a carefully programmed computer and a sophisticated probe, he has the ability to identify crew and children who have no counterparts in the other universe."

They all sat in silence, digesting what Ambassador Kaner told them. Gerroll spoke first. "That would make sense. According to the research done on parallel universes, like entities cannot exist together for long periods in the same universe. This commander may be bad, but he is very ingenious."

"That would also explain the girls' presence," Marsh said. "They have no counterparts in this universe." It was all coming together like the pieces of a puzzle.

"There is one thing that does not match," Kaner said.

"What is that, Ambassador?" Gerroll asked.

"All of the children kidnapped were infants. Your girls are older," Kaner answered.

"Infants are easier to transport and have no memory of where they came from," Gerroll explained.

"Then why the girls?" Wells mused.

"There are other reasons for kidnapping," Gerroll reminded him.

"That's true," Wells said and turned to Marsh. "Let's face it, Bill. You've got a lot of enemies in this universe, especially the Frazons! If your counterpart is anything like you, I'm sure he does too."

Marsh stared out the window, looking at the beautiful sky while contemplating such ugly deeds. "To my knowledge, we've never encountered the Mog. But they live in Frazon space, and we have had some run-ins with the Frazons. The worst was when a Frazon ship was destroyed during a battle with the Polaris. We have to assume the other Polaris, in the other universe, had the same experience. Someone in that other universe is seeking revenge for the destruction of that Frazon ship," he guessed.

"Or revenge for the loss of someone on it," Wells suggested.

"A child for a child, perhaps?" Kaner said, and they all looked at him.

"Yes," Marsh repeated softly, nodding his head, "or two children for a child." He thought of the two sleeping girls the night before and the unexpected emotions he had felt. He stood up abruptly, and his officers followed him.

"One last question, Ambassador," Marsh said. "Did the prisoner say where in Frazon space the portal to this other universe is located?"

Kaner thought for a moment before answering. "He said the Mog ship had been disabled and had drifted into uncharted territory. There were only a few inhabited planets and no space stations to help them. They drifted through a nebula, expecting it to be like any other cloud of dust and gas, but instead of ending up on the other side, they ended up in another universe. He said it wasn't too far from our outposts—just on the other side of the boundary line—in Frazon space."

"Where exactly are your outposts located?" Gerroll asked.

"I will have the coordinates sent directly to your computers," Kaner promised.

Marsh shook Kaner's hand, as did Gerroll and Wells.

"Thank you, Ambassador Kaner," Marsh said. "You have no idea what a help you've been. At least now we have a place to start."

"Captain, please let me know what happens," Kaner said.

"We will, Ambassador. In the meantime, keep your fingers crossed." Marsh pressed his communication badge. "Three to transport up."

Marsh waited for Ambassador Kaner to transmit the coordinates of the Sarasian outposts, the whole time wondering how he was going to explain the situation to Space Central. If what Kaner said was true, they would have to cross into Frazon space to search for the portal that would bring them into the girls' home universe.

Marsh turned to the sound of the hyperlift doors opening and watched Dr. Wells approach his command chair. "Have you met the girls, Matt?" Marsh asked him.

"Not yet. I wanted to get caught up in the sickbay first. Kate told me they are great kids. She's really enjoying them. And so is Jared! It seems that Jared's counterpart is a good friend of the girls in their universe. They make a great trio."

"Good, I'm glad the girls have company. Call them down to the sickbay and give them a quick physical. I'm sure they're fine, but they haven't had any medical attention since they were abducted."

"Yes, I was thinking the same thing."

"Good. And, Matt, keep me informed."

Gerroll interrupted them. "The coordinates are coming in from Saras, Captain."

Wells left to find his patients, and Marsh crossed the bridge to the science station.

"Here, Captain, take a look," Gerroll said. The layout of the Frazon boundary line was holographically displayed above his station, and he pointed to the position of the outposts where the kidnappings had occurred. "These are the five outposts. Right here along the Frazon border. And this area," he circled a section with his finger, "is where I estimate the portal to the other universe would be. The ambassador said the Mog ship had been disabled and had drifted into an area of space where they were unable to get any assistance. As you can see by what information we have—and keep in mind that our information on this region of space is limited—there are very few, if any, inhabitable planets, and no space stations."

Marsh nodded as he listened. "We have no other choice. That's where we'll start. How long will it take to get there?"

"By my calculations, two days, seven hours. At top speed."

Marsh turned his attention to his communications officer. "Lieutenant Diska, contact Admiral Packard at Space Central and transfer her down to my quarters."

"Yes, Sir."

"Gerroll, if I can convince Space Central to let us

cross into Frazon space for this, I think I could do just about anything!"

"And if they say 'No?'"

Marsh shrugged. "Get used to being called 'Daddy,' I guess. I'll be in my quarters."

Dr. Wells found the girls in the corridor outside their quarters and was surprised by their reaction to him. Diane and Robin fell into step next to him, chatting enthusiastically as if they had known him forever. He laughed when he realized that in their universe, his counterpart *had* known them forever.

Wells examined the girls as they chatted and found them to be in good health. They were, for obvious reasons, stressed, and both were slightly vitamin deficient. Nothing serious. One dose by a pressure injector would take care of the deficiency, which would also help their stress levels.

It might have helped their stress levels, but it certainly didn't help his. He'd never heard so much fuss over one small injector. He was used to dealing with children, the Polaris had one hundred ninety-two aboard, including his own child, but this was ridiculous. The girls protested so loudly, one of the nurses came in from the next room to see what all the noise was about. She leaned against the wall and watched, thoroughly amused by the unfolding scene.

"You *could* help me out here, Nurse Russen," Wells yelled over to her, but she was laughing too hard to be of any assistance.

He finally gave up and let the girls go. When they left, he called the captain to give him the requested update.

"Marsh here. How did it go, Matt? They okay?"

"Yes, they're fine, Bill. A little vitamin deficient and stressed, but okay."

"You gave them something for it?"

"Well, no. They weren't exactly thrilled about the injector and I…um…I let it go."

"What's the problem, Matt? You're the doctor. If they need an injection, just give it to them," Marsh said bluntly.

You *give it,* I'll *watch,* Wells thought.

CHAPTER 22

A TINY SPIDER

MARSH WAS SITTING in his quarters, having spent another sleepless night contemplating the possibilities of his daughters' whereabouts. His intercom buzzed. It was Lieutenant Helen Diska.

"Captain, I have Dr. Wells for you. He's in Ambassador Kaner's office and he says it's urgent that he speak with you."

"Transfer it down here, Lieutenant."

"Yes, Sir. One moment."

"Bill?"

"Yes, Matt. What is it?" Marsh leaned his head against his hand and wondered what the urgency was. Wells was finishing up on Saras this morning and should be transporting back to the ship shortly.

"I was telling Ambassador Kaner about the girls, and he says he might be able to help. I think you should hear his theory."

"I'm on my way," Marsh said immediately, thankful for any help he could get. He pressed the intercom button to reconnect to the bridge. "Lieutenant Diska, have Gerroll meet me in the transporter room at once. We're transporting down to Saras."

"Yes, Sir. He's on his way now."

Marsh headed for the transporter room and maybe, just maybe, he would learn something that would bring him closer to hearing the girls' laughter again.

They materialized on the planet surface and Marsh looked up. He had never seen such a beautiful sky…

When they returned to the Polaris, Marsh sat impatiently in his command chair while Gerroll waited for the coordinates of the Sarasian outposts on the boundary line. He thought about the theory Ambassador Kaner had presented to them. It was an incredible story, but he knew better than to count it out. He hated to admit that it even made sense. Wells was probably correct in his assumption that revenge was at work here, maybe even a child for a child. The thought made him shudder. Was he really being held responsible for the death of someone on that Frazon warship? Was it really his fault?

No. It had been war. The Frazons attacked first. They crossed the boundary line and attacked LUP outposts. Innocent people had been killed. Marsh had been protecting what was his sworn duty to protect—his ship, his crew, LUP territory, and his children. Always, his children.

In the battle, Marsh had finally outwitted and outmaneuvered the Frazon commander, but in doing so, five of his own crewmembers had been killed. And still, Marsh had offered the Frazon commander life. He had offered to transport the remainder of the defeated crew aboard the Polaris, but that was not the Frazon way. Instead, the Frazon commander chose to continue the hopeless fight. He had tried to fire one last torpedo at the Polaris, but due to the damage his ship had sustained during the battle, the torpedo misfired and the Frazon ship destroyed itself, along with its crew.

Come on Kaner…transmit those damn coordinates, Marsh thought, his impatience growing by the second.

Marsh felt a tickle on the back of his neck and touched it with his hand. There was something there. He scooped it up and held his hand open to see what it was. A tiny spider sat in the center of his palm. It must have fallen from a tree while he was on Saras. He sat mesmerized by this little defenseless creature. Yet another thing that reminded him of his girls.

It was 2100 hours and Marsh was surprised to see Diane come into the main lounge. She didn't hesitate, even though the room was now closed to the children. She was dressed in gray sweats, gray socks, and no shoes—her favorite after-school attire—but she should be in her quarters getting ready to call it a day. He'd be in to say good night within the hour, and she could have spoken to him then. But he had an inkling that something was going on, and he wanted to know what it was.

Diane didn't need to scan the room. She knew just where her father would be seated—in front of the viewing window that covered the entire front wall of the main lounge, resting in the chair that no one else ever dared sit in. It was one of those big couch-like chairs that at least two people could fit into. For one person, it was like sitting on a cloud, and once you sat down you never wanted to get up. Diane should know—it was secretly her and Robin's favorite place to talk and read when their father wasn't in it. As expected, that's where he was, and Dr. Wells was sitting across from him.

She didn't ask his permission to stay; she just sat down and leaned against him, tucking her legs under her. His arm was resting over the top of the chair, and she snuggled into the comfortable space between his arm and chest. She put her head down on his shoulder and waited for him to finish the conversation he was having with Dr. Wells, who seemed to understand that this must be an important chat she was waiting to have.

"I've got to finish up in the lab, Bill. I'll see you in the morning," Wells said and winked at Diane.

"'Night, Matt," Marsh said to his friend.

"Good night, Diane," Wells added as he passed and patted her on the head.

"Good night, Dr. Wells," she said and smiled up at him in appreciation of his departure.

Marsh turned his concentration to his daughter. "I gather you want to talk to me."

She didn't answer, but Marsh could feel her head moving up and down on his chest as she nodded.

"What's up?"

"I don't want to go on the field trip with the class tomorrow," she said matter-of-factly. "I told Lieutenant Carin that, but she said I had to get your permission to stay behind."

Having met the lieutenant in the corridor on his way to the lounge, he already knew about Diane's request, but Lieutenant Carin also said that Diane wouldn't give a reason for not wanting to go…she had just simply stated that she wouldn't be joining the rest of the class.

"How come?" Marsh inquired. "You like going down to new planets and you love plants. Lieutenant Carin said the reason for this excursion is to study the flora and vegetation. The exploration teams have informed me that the planet is lovely."

"There are other things down there I don't like and I'm not going."

Marsh couldn't see her face, but her voice was adamant. Now he understood. He'd heard about the 'other things' too.

"They're not spiders, Diane. They are called Baract-das, and they are indigenous to the planet."

"Well, they look like spiders and they're big. I'm not going!" she shouted.

Marsh's oldest daughter had a serious fear of spiders. When she was younger, he assumed that she would outgrow it, but she never did. She wouldn't even remain in the same room if she knew a spider was there.

It always amazed him that she never found a spider in the middle of the afternoon, but at 0300 hours in the morning, there was always one around. His girls rarely had *nightmares, so if Diane was waking him up, a spider was surely close by. He always tried logic first. "They're more afraid of you than you are of them," he would tell her, but his dialectic never worked. She would drag him out of a nice, warm bed and into her room, point to a tiny, harmless spider huddled in the corner of the ceiling and cry, "Kill it, Daddy! Kill it!" She wouldn't be happy until he annihilated every spider in the universe. Then Robin would come in, awakened by the noise, screaming at him, "Don't kill it, Daddy! Take it outside!"*

So, in the middle of the night, he would have to take the spider outside to appease Robin, but make sure it was far enough away so Diane would be convinced it wouldn't crawl back with its friends and family to find her. At least on the Polaris there weren't many spiders. But rest assured, when one did show up, with an entire ship to choose from, it somehow always managed to find Diane's quarters. And always in the middle of the night.

Marsh didn't understand Diane's fear, but he respected it. Everyone wrestled with something they were afraid of and she was no exception. On one hand, he didn't want to force her to do something she was scared of. But on the other hand, he didn't want her missing a school assignment because of it.

"Who's your partner for the expedition?" he asked, as if he didn't already know.

"Robin," she answered, confirming his assumption.

"How about if we pair Robin up with Lieutenant Carin and we get you a new partner?" he suggested.

"There is no one else. It doesn't matter. I don't want to

go!" she yelled. He could hear the panic in her voice and she had started to cry.

"Don't cry. I'm trying to help." Then a little softer, "I know you're scared."

"Who then?" she asked doubtfully.

"Me. I'll go with you."

"You said at dinner that you were going to be super busy tomorrow."

"I am, but I'll make different arrangements and ask Gerroll to cover for me while I'm gone."

"You have to do all of the digging," Diane said between sniffles. "I heard the members of the exploration teams say that those things were under the dirt. I won't do any digging. I won't."

Marsh could feel her tremble at the thought. "Okay, I'll do the digging, but you have to do everything else. I know it won't help to tell you this, but they are harmless and more scared of you than you are of them. Really!"

Diane didn't care. "You'll kill them?" she asked pleadingly.

"No, being afraid of something is not a reason to kill it. But I'll keep them out of your way."

"Promise?"

"Yes, I promise."

"You'll protect me?"

"Yes."

"Swear?"

"Don't I always?" he asked as he tickled his daughter's shoulder. She giggled in response to his teasing.

"Yes," she answered and then added, "But I'd be much happier if you just blew up the whole planet."

Being a father was a tough job.

Marsh carefully put the spider on the floor. Robin would be happy. Diane wouldn't be. But now nothing would please him more than to wake up in the middle of the night to see Diane standing at his bedside begging him to come and save her from the big, bad spider.

"Coordinates coming in, Captain," Gerroll informed him. Finally.

"Can you get a fix on the locations of the outposts?" Marsh asked.

"Completed, Captain."

Marsh walked over to Gerroll's science station. "Plot a course. How long will it take us to get there?"

"Two days, seven hours. At top speed."

"Well, I have that long to convince Space Central to allow us to cross into Frazon space." Marsh turned his head in the direction of the communications station.

"Lieutenant Diska, contact Admiral Packard at Space Central and transfer her down to my quarters."

"Yes, Sir."

Gerroll leaned closer to him. "What will you do if they refuse, Bill?"

"I won't let them refuse. I can't."

Marsh left the bridge and prepped himself for the most difficult request he'd ever made, but he knew it didn't matter what the answer was. He was going anyway.

Marsh carefully watched Admiral Packard's face on the viewscreen while he filled her in on the events that had taken place since their last conversation when he had told the admiral about the girls' abduction. Admiral Samantha Packard had been one of his instructors at the Academy, and they had become, if not exactly friends, mutual admirers. She had even met the girls on numerous occasions, but Marsh knew none of that would influence her decision.

"Captain, nothing would give me more pleasure than to immediately grant your request. I have children and grandchildren of my own, so I understand what you are feeling. I am not, however, in a position to do that. Let me speak to Space Central on your behalf. I will give you their decision by 1800 hours."

Officially, Packard had said what she had to say. Unofficially, she asked, "Bill, what if they say 'No?'" They both knew it was a strong possibility.

"Gerroll asked me the same question, Admiral. I'll tell you what I told him. I won't accept 'No' for an answer. I can't. You know that. You said it yourself… you have children and grandchildren. What would you do if the situation were reversed?"

Packard didn't hesitate before answering. "I understand. I'll do what I can. Packard out."

Now Marsh had something else to wait for. It seemed as if the waiting never ended these days.

CHAPTER 23

PIZZA PIES...AGAIN

Marsh sat at his desk in front of the viewscreen and watched the admiral's surprised expression. "That's the whole story, Admiral."

"And quite a story it is. I wish I had the authority to say 'Yes,' Captain, but I don't. Let me take it up with Space Central and I'll get back to you by 1800 hours."

"Thank you, Admiral. I'd appreciate any help you can give us."

"What will you do with the girls if you can't get them back home?"

"My parents want to raise them."

Packard chuckled. "Until you can take them?" She paused when she noticed Marsh wasn't laughing with her. "Sorry, Captain. I don't mean to make light of the situation, but I've got kids and grandkids. It's a wonderful experience. Your counterpart was able to convince Space Central to allow commanders to bring children aboard, so perhaps we can do the same for you under the circumstances."

Marsh didn't comment on the admiral's remarks. "Please do what you can, Admiral. I'll speak with you later." Somehow, this conversation didn't amuse him.

"Okay, '*Dad!*' Packard out."

Despite her warm smile, Marsh hoped Packard wasn't trying to tell him something.

The bridge was quiet. It was going to be a long afternoon. The Polaris was headed for the Frazon boundary line even though they didn't have permission from Space Central yet. It would be a few more hours until he heard from Packard. Marsh would have loved to be a fly on *that* wall! It must be some discussion they were having. Gerroll was busy at his science station and Wells was filling him in on his weeks on Saras.

"Captain," Lieutenant Diska interrupted, "we just received a message from Space Central."

"Packard?" Marsh questioned with surprise. "I wasn't expecting to hear from her for a few hours yet."

"No, Sir. It's not Admiral Packard."

"Oh. What does it say?"

"Well, Sir, it says that…um…there are reports of numerous, unauthorized distress calls coming from the Polaris."

"Distress calls, Lieutenant? Are you sure? We haven't sent any distress calls. What are they for?"

"Calls for emergency deliveries, Sir, and they said

to remind you that the unauthorized use of a distress signal is against Space Central regulations."

"I know that. What kind of deliveries, Lieutenant."

No way, Diska thought, *I'm not telling him.*

"LIEUTENANT!"

"Pizza pies, Sir."

No one dared move or say a word. Marsh jumped up and headed for the hyperlift and, as he entered, the only sound he could hear was Gerroll's laughter.

CHAPTER 24

DAD WAITS

THE AFTERNOON SEEMED to go on forever. No one knew what to say to Marsh, so no one talked to him except Gerroll and Matt Wells. The safest place for Marsh was the bridge, where he could bury himself in his work and not run headfirst into thoughts of his daughters.

They kept on the course that had been set for the Frazon border. Gerroll had provided his best guess on where the portal would be, and that's where they were headed. Marsh would worry about how to handle the situation when, and if, Space Central denied his request. Until then, he would continue to be optimistic.

Matt stayed by Marsh's side as if afraid to leave him and filled him in on every little detail of his time on Saras until Marsh felt he had been there himself. At times, Marsh wanted to scream, "Enough already," but he let Wells talk and tried his best to concentrate. Marsh suspected what his friend was doing and was grateful.

Gerroll looked over every now and then and was glad that Wells was keeping the captain, and his thoughts, occupied.

"Captain," Lieutenant Diska interrupted, speaking very softly, "I have Admiral Packard for you. Do you want to take it here or in your quarters?"

Marsh was about to say that he would speak to the admiral in his quarters, but realized that his bridge crew needed to hear this conversation. If Space Central denied his request, as they probably would, and he made the decision to go anyway, as he knew he would, then his crew deserved to hear their captain's decision. "Here, Lieutenant. Put it on visual."

Admiral Packard's face materialized on the big viewing screen in front of him. Marsh was nervous and he discreetly wiped his sweating palms on the sides of his pants.

"Captain Marsh," Packard said in greeting.

"Admiral," Marsh replied.

"Well, Captain, it seems you have a guardian angel sitting on your shoulder."

Marsh didn't understand the remark, but assumed it meant good news. "Admiral?"

"Ambassador Kaner contacted Space Central on your behalf. He wanted us to know how pleased he was with Dr. Wells's performance. Their epidemic is under control. Then he requested that you be allowed the chance to capture the criminals who terrorized the Sasarian outposts and kidnapped their children. He felt it was in the LUP's best interest to keep this from happening again. We agree with him. Go find your girls, Captain, and find the people responsible. But, and this is vital, Captain—*don't* start a war with the Frazons in the process."

A Saras fairy, indeed! For a moment, Marsh was speechless. He was afraid if he spoke, his emotions would betray him. He nodded slowly, and when he was sure of his composure, he allowed himself to respond. "Thank you, Admiral. We'll do our best not to start any wars!"

Packard smiled at him. "Good luck, Captain. Packard out."

When the connection was broken, the bridge was quiet. The silence didn't last long, though. Within seconds, the entire bridge crew broke into applause and cheers.

Marsh and Gerroll spent the next few hours deep in conversation, planning strategies and discussing possibilities. Marsh picked at dinner, which a yeoman brought to him on Matt Wells's orders. He hadn't really eaten in days, and he couldn't remember the last time he slept. It didn't matter. Finding his girls was all that mattered now.

The ship's chief medical officer had a different view on the subject. "That's it, Bill," Wells announced as he walked off the hyperlift. He stood next to his friend and whispered into his ear: "Either you go voluntarily and get some sleep, or I'm going to give you something that will make you sleep. Either way, you're leaving the bridge…now. Your choice. My orders."

Marsh rubbed his temples, aware that Wells was right. He couldn't help feeling, however, that if he slept he would lose precious time.

"I'm not kidding, Captain," Wells said officially. "Make a choice or I will make it for you." Wells held up a pressure injector and Marsh realized his friend was serious.

Marsh raised his hands to surrender. "Okay, Matt. I'll go. On my own. No injector, thank you." He wanted to be alert in case he was needed. "Gerroll, I'll be in my quarters."

Gerroll nodded in affirmation, thankful that Wells had pressed the issue. The second-in-command and doctor smiled at each other in triumph as Marsh entered the hyperlift.

Marsh had been lying on his bed for what seemed an eternity, exhausted but unable to sleep. Maybe he should have let Wells give him something after all. He tried to clear his mind, but it was impossible. The girls were there, in every thought and every breath.

It took hours of tossing and turning, but at last he fell into a deep sleep, his thoughts finally given a reprieve from the horrors his imagination was conjuring up. He couldn't bear to think what his innocent daughters were going through.

CHAPTER 25

FATHERHOOD

"No, Uncle Bill, it's not fair!" Robin screamed. "We were only having fun!"

"We won't do it again," Diane continued. "We won't. Promise."

"I'm quite sure of *that*," Marsh said. He had ordered pizza for dinner, his original anger having faded when he realized the prank really *was* funny. Besides, the good news from Admiral Packard that Space Central would allow them to cross into Frazon space, thanks to the help of Ambassador Kaner, had also helped to brighten his mood. Still, the girls had gone where they weren't allowed and, when dinner was over, he had ordered them to their quarters for the remainder of the night.

The girls liked the pizza, but obviously, not the penalty. They were standing next to his chair in his private dining room and, much to his anger and dismay, insisted on continuing the argument.

"We are going to the rec room tonight to see the holomovie being shown," Diane insisted.

"No, you're going to your quarters," Marsh said again. He was rapidly losing his patience.

Jared watched in astonishment. No one, but no one, argued with Captain Marsh, especially not any of the kids. He couldn't help but smile, however, and secretly hoped that Diane and Robin would win the battle. What a coup that would be! None of the other kids were going to believe this!

Matt and Kate Wells were also enjoying the scene immensely. It was a rare treat to see Bill Marsh in a situation that got the better of him, at least for the moment.

Gerroll was watching too, eagerly waiting to see who emerged victorious, although he had no doubt who it would be.

The girls raged on.

"No, we don't want to go to our quarters. It's boring there. We don't have any of the things we have on our Polaris," Robin griped.

Marsh wondered how his counterpart would have handled this situation, but he had the feeling this wouldn't happen in their universe. He was certain he was being tested, and he was going to make sure it didn't happen again. He watched the girls with narrowed eyes while they continued to argue, surprised they hadn't sensed his mounting anger.

"We'll go to the rec room and *then* we'll go to our quarters," Diane told him.

That's it. He'd had enough. He didn't repeat orders more than once, let alone twice. Without warning, Marsh abruptly stood up, his chair rattling behind him.

Shocked silence.

Marsh said nothing, knowing that silence was often more powerful than words. The girls watched him, not sure what he was going to do. He let them wonder for a few seconds. One thing was certain—he would not repeat the command.

"Now…*where* are you going?" he asked them, so softly they had to strain to hear him.

"Our quarters," they said in stereo, matching the softness of his tone.

Marsh smiled and nodded his head. "I'll stop in later to say good night," he told them as he retook his seat.

Diane and Robin said their good nights, and then, much to his surprise, each gave him a quick peck on his cheek. They left defeated. He watched them go, shaking his head.

Jared got up and quickly followed the girls out of the dining room. He couldn't wait to congratulate them on their valiant effort.

Matt Wells was staring at Marsh, obviously impressed.

"What's the matter, Matt?"

"Nothing, Bill." He paused and pondered the simplicity of the captain's solution. "Your solution was… perfect."

"Yes, Bill," Kate added. "You're really doing very well under the circumstances!"

"I agree, Captain," Gerroll said. "I noticed, however, that you didn't say anything to the girls about the information we learned today from Ambassador Kaner."

"I decided against it for now. I don't want to get their hopes up. When we know more and are sure we can get them home, then I'll tell them. For now I think it's best they think this is where they'll be staying."

"Well, it seems that you're certainly getting the hang of fatherhood rather quickly," Matt said, smiling.

"I don't have much of a choice. It's what you call a real crash course!" Marsh looked around the table. "Thank you all for your words of encouragement. I'm going back to the bridge."

They all watched as Marsh headed for the door. No one moved. Marsh turned and looked at his still-seated officers. He smiled at them. "Do I need to send you to your quarters, also, or are you going to your posts?" he asked them.

Uncertain whether or not Marsh was serious, Matt stammered, "Um…our posts, Captain. We're going to our posts."

The officers rose and followed their commanding officer out the door, each now quite certain that Marsh had indeed gotten the hang of fatherhood.

CHAPTER 26

DAD, I KNOW WHAT I WANT TO BE

MARSH HAD TO admit that Wells was right. A good night's sleep was just what he had needed. That, coupled with the news that they were free to cross the boundary line had made the morning easier to face.

Catching up from his time away was still one of his main priorities, but this morning, even that could wait. Instead, Marsh decided to do an inspection of the entire ship. It was long overdue, and it would keep him busy for hours. It would also give him peace of mind knowing that everyone and everything was ready to face whatever happened in the next few days. He needed his crew alert and all systems in perfect order. He went from department to department and was happy to see things running smoothly and to his expectations. He also ran into memories everywhere he went, and it seemed as if Diane and Robin were doing the inspection with him.

But that was okay, his brighter feeling made it a little easier to cope.

When he passed the girls' quarters, he hesitated, then went in and sat there for a while. He sat quietly, as he had the day before—and probably would every day until they returned—and remembered. It seemed as if there were an infinite number of memories, and his heart tightened with each one as it surfaced.

Marsh reflected, as he often did, even before their abduction, about the girls' entry into his life. He loved them as if they were his own, and he sometimes forgot that they weren't. He made sure the girls knew they could talk to him at any time about their parents. When they questioned him about Daniel and Beth, he told them what he knew and, what he didn't know, he found out for them.

One thing he knew was that Beth had loved to sing. He remembered when he had visited how she would walk around the house with a song always on her lips. She had had a lovely voice, and he had loved to listen. The girls also liked to sing, and he loved listening to them, too, when they let him, which wasn't often.

They sang mostly for themselves, doing arrangements that Robin figured out from popular and old songs. When they thought the corridors were empty, they'd sing and harmonize as they walked, enjoying the great acoustics of the open space. Sitting in their quarters now, he could almost hear the melodies. He could also hear the yelling, arguing, and frustration that came with raising children. As nice as it would be if life were always peaceful, he knew from experience that was not the case! And yet, he missed that too.

Somehow, with them gone, it seemed so trivial that he had gotten angry over such small things as their messy quarters, cutting classes, and teenage cockiness. But he knew that when they came back, and they *would* come back, they would argue about these issues all over again. It was all part of the process.

Marsh drank in what he could of them, and then continued on his inspection. One of the last places he visited was the geology lab. It was hard not to see Robin there, his geologist in the making.

It would take only a few hours to complete this mission. The planet was seemingly barren of any sapient life entities, and they were there to do various inhabitability studies.

Marsh didn't need to transport down with the exploration team, but it was a good excuse to bring the girls down for sunshine and fresh air. They walked together for awhile and then he let the girls wander off by themselves, as long as they stayed within eyeshot. The rule was "look, but don't touch anything," and they practically walked with their hands in their pockets. But that was okay by them—it was fun just being allowed to go.

After exploring on their own a little, the girls returned to stay with their father. Gradually, the exploration team filtered back with their preliminary reports. Within two hours, they were back on the ship, the balance of the work to be done by the ship's computers and the individual labs. Marsh would have the finished reports by the end of the day.

Upon arrival back on the ship, Marsh checked with Gerroll and found everything to be running smoothly. An hour or two in his office would help bring some of his own reports under control. He'd barely begun when Robin entered, looking a little nervous and unsure. He didn't ask any questions; he knew she'd get to the point when she was ready.

"I had a nice time today," she told him as she sat down.

"Good, I'm glad." He leaned back, folded his hands on the desk, and smiled at her. He was ready to listen if she was ready to talk.

"Daddy, I was wondering if…just this once…maybe I could go to the geology lab while they work up the finished reports for you. I promise not to get in the way. I just want to listen." She hesitated and added, "Please?"

Marsh never let the girls interfere with ship's business and he thought very carefully about her request. He knew how much she loved rocks and minerals—she had since she'd been old enough to hold them.

"Why?" he asked.

"I thought the report Lieutenant Aldridge gave you about the planet was really interesting. I wanted to hear the rest of it and how she came to her conclusions."

"I see. You really do enjoy geology, don't you?"

Her face lit up. "Yes!"

Simple answer to a simple question, yet she seemed uneasy again. He didn't have to wait long to find out what was on her mind.

"Daddy, I was thinking that I might want to be a geologist someday."

"I think that's a wonderful idea, Robin."

"You do?" she asked in disbelief.

"Why wouldn't I?" he asked, surprised that she thought he would answer to the contrary.

"I love collecting rocks and researching all about them. But when it comes to the real study of geology, I'm not sure I can do it. Math and science aren't my best subjects. You know that."

"What's important, Robin, is that you love what you do. If you choose to make a career out of something, you will be doing it for a long time."

"I do love it."

"Then don't worry about the math and science. You'll have to work harder at them and maybe get some extra help along the way, but your love of geology will get you through. And I'll be there to help any way I can. You're a very smart girl, Robin. You can do whatever you want to do. I have faith in you."

She smiled up at him. As always, he encouraged her to follow her heart.

Marsh tapped his communication badge. "Lieutenant Aldridge, I'm sending my daughter Robin down to the geology lab. As long as she follows the rules, let her stay as long as she wants." He looked up and saw the unabashed joy on Robin's face. "And please answer any questions that she has. Marsh out." He turned to his youngest child. "Okay?"

Her hug said it all.

CHAPTER 27

THE DREADED INJECTOR

According to Gerroll, they were still twenty-six hours and eight minutes from the boundary line. There was little they could do but wait. Then they would cross into unknown territory and would have to feel their way.

The girls questioned Marsh often about going home, but he answered vaguely, not wanting to give them false hope. He knew they were homesick. Luckily, though, the children on the ship did everything possible to make the girls feel at home. Still, they were restless.

He, on the other hand, had a lot on his agenda. He spent some time going over computer logs, and then spent a couple of hours with Kate in engineering, making sure everything was in tip-top shape just in case they had any run-ins with the Frazons once they crossed the boundary line.

In the meantime, the crew was doing combat exercises, over and over, until he was satisfied that they were performing to his expectations. Gerroll was concerned, as he was, that the Frazons wouldn't be their only problem. Both had been expecting the Mog commander to try to abduct the girls again, and were surprised that an attempt had not already been made. Marsh didn't believe for one second that the Mog had given up so easily. He had been mulling over an idea and stopped in the sickbay to discuss it with Dr. Wells. The doctor listened intently, and then nodded his head in agreement.

"It will take me a few minutes to prepare. You get the girls down here. And Bill, stick around. I'm not doing this alone."

"Scared of two girls, Matt?"

"Yes."

Marsh laughed and paged his communications officer. "Lieutenant Diska, please locate Diane and Robin and have them report to the sickbay at once."

"Yes, Captain."

It took only moments before the girls entered the sickbay, very slowly and quite timidly.

Nurse Russen greeted them at the door. "Dr. Wells would like to see you. He's in there," she told them, and pointed to the back room of the sickbay. She was having a conversation with the captain who acknowledged the girls with his eyes and a smile while he continued to talk.

Diane and Robin eyed him suspiciously as they passed, but didn't interrupt him. Wells met them as soon as they entered.

"Captain wants you to have those vitamin shots you didn't get."

"Why?" Diane asked. The girls had been so relieved to avoid the dreaded injectors in the first place.

"Go ask the captain. I'm just following orders," Dr. Wells replied. The girls watched unhappily as he prepared the pressure injector.

"Can't it wait until tomorrow, or the next day, or the day after that?" Diane asked pleadingly, desperate to avoid an injection.

"Like I said, go ask him," Dr. Wells repeated and nodded in Marsh's direction. The girls followed his gaze, but neither moved. Marsh was still deep in conversation with Nurse Russen.

"Good idea, Diane. Go ask him," Robin said.

"I'm not asking him. You ask him."

"Nope. Not me."

Dr. Wells looked from one to the other. "Well, that's settled. Who's first?"

Diane quickly pushed her sister forward. "She is."

"No, she is." Robin retaliated.

"Who's older?" he asked, catching them off guard.

"Me," Diane answered without thinking.

"Thank you for volunteering," he said and took her arm.

"No!" Diane started to protest. She glanced at Marsh, whose head had snapped up from the commotion. One look at his stern expression and she realized this battle was lost. Nothing left to do but bite the bullet. She turned her arm toward Dr. Wells, her head in the opposite direction so she wouldn't have to watch, and braced for the sting. "I hate that thing!" she complained loudly and rubbed her arm while Robin took her turn.

"All over. Now that wasn't so bad, was it?" the doctor asked.

"YES, it was!" Diane screamed.

"Next time, I'll use a hypodermic needle instead," he proposed. "Trust me, you'll never complain about a pressure injector again."

"What's a hypodermic needle?" Robin asked him.

He went to a drawer, searched until he found what he was looking for, and gave it to them for closer inspection.

Diane turned it over in her hands. "Oh, wow, look at that needle. What's it used for?"

"That's what was used until the end of the twenty-first century when the pressure injector was invented," Dr. Wells answered, enjoying the look of alarm on their faces.

"No, really," Robin said, taking it from her sister and inspecting it more closely.

"Really!" he said, and paused to let the information sink in. "And if either of you ever give me a problem again…"

Wells was sure they paled at least two shades.

Having finished his conversation, Marsh joined the trio. "All done, Matt?"

"Yes, Captain."

Marsh looked at the hypodermic needle and smiled. "Nasty thing," he said. "Had one once."

"You did?" Diane asked, not sure if she should believe him.

"Yep. Years ago on Lumar V. Got bit by a curicca bug and I needed the antidote immediately. I didn't even have time to get back to my ship, and those needles were all their doctors had."

"Did it…did it…hurt?" Robin asked, almost afraid to hear the answer.

"Much more than a pressure injector. Wasn't crazy about where they put it, either," he said and patted his butt.

The girls looked at him, at Dr. Wells, and then each other.

"I'm going back to the bridge. Would you two like to come?" he asked. The least he could do was offer them a consolation prize.

Still flexing their sore arms and contemplating the horrors of the hypodermic needle, the sisters nodded and followed him out of the sickbay.

The bridge was quiet. Marsh settled into his command chair, comfortable, at home. The girls took a seat on either side of him, perched on the edge of the platform that raised his chair above everyone else's.

"Status report," Marsh asked.

"Nothing unusual to report," his second-in-command replied.

"Good, Gerroll. Let's try to keep it that way." Wishful thinking, he knew. The quiet on the Polaris never lasted very long, and probably wouldn't this time, considering their present predicament. But it was welcome when it came. Very welcome.

Marsh sat back, crossed his legs, and watched the viewscreen. As the stars slipped silently past, he felt a rare peace fill him. Every once in a while, he would look down at the two girls sitting next to him and was amazed how content they looked. They had explained to him that their father only allowed them on the bridge when everything was quiet and, even then, only for a short time. A rule Marsh completely agreed with, but he was glad he could give them an infrequent treat. All things considered, they'd been very good.

Robin's voice distracted his thoughts. "Uncle Bill?"

"Yes?"

"Is it true that the Polaris is the most requested assignment in Space Central?"

"That's what they tell me."

"Do you get to choose which candidates you want?" Diane asked.

"Sometimes. Why?"

"There's a man on the list, Lieutenant Ben Farber," Robin explained. "He's the man who helped us on the transport vessel. The one who transported us down to the ranch. Do you think you could do something to help him?"

"Anything is possible. Maybe I can repay his help," he replied, and made a mental note to contact Space Central.

"Thank you," Diane and Robin said together.

"Captain," Gerroll urgently called out to him. "Ship materializing on the starboard side."

Materializing? A camouflaged ship? On this side of the boundary line? Frazon? Or Mog?

The quiet on the Polaris had just ended.

CHAPTER 28

CAPTURED

"We are being probed, Captain," Gerroll informed him as he continued his scanning. "By what I believe to be the Mog ship."

Marsh frowned. Finally. He'd been waiting. "Priority 1 alert!" he stated loudly.

At that precise moment, Dr. Wells entered from the hyperlift and started toward the captain's chair. Marsh rose and grabbed each girl who were clinging to the sides of his chair in terror. "Matt, get them off the bridge!" Marsh shouted and pushed both girls at once in Wells's direction. But it was too late. Before Wells could take another step, the girls disappeared into the glow of a transporter beam.

"NO!" Marsh yelled and leaped toward their last position as if he could stop the transporter beam merely with his presence. But they were gone.

Marsh started issuing orders. "Ensign Todd, raise

shields! Lieutenant Walker, target phasers!" He gave Walker the few seconds he needed and then yelled, "FIRE!"

"Captain, we're being hailed," Lieutenant Diska told him.

"Matt, quickly!" Marsh said and Wells rushed to his side. "I didn't get a chance to advise Gerroll. Tell him what to look for."

"Put it on the viewscreen, Lieutenant Diska," Marsh ordered and turned to the large screen.

The bridge of the Mog ship appeared and, in the center of the screen was, who Marsh assumed to be, the Mog commander. The girls had been right, he *was* big... and ugly, with bulging metallic-gold eyes, huge facial features, and long, black hair pulled back and reminiscent of a horse's tail, which reached the middle of his black tunic. He had each girl on either side of him—in a headlock. Marsh's breathing quickened when he saw the look of fear on their young faces.

"Hold your fire, Captain, or I will break their necks." For effect, the Mog commander tightened his hold on the girls, and they shrieked.

Diane and Robin looked so small next to the Mog's huge body, Marsh thought. Small and frightened. "Hold your fire, Lieutenant Walker," Marsh commanded, his eyes never leaving the viewscreen.

Marsh knew the Mog was bluffing. The commander needed the girls, and he needed them alive or he wouldn't have come back for them. But Marsh wasn't about to take any chances.

The commander released his hold on the girls, just a little, and Marsh could see the girls relax, just a little. Marsh held up his hands as if to surrender. "We won't fire. Let them go."

"Let them go? I don't think so, Captain Marsh. They escaped from me once. They won't do it again."

It surprised Marsh to be called by name. "You have me at a disadvantage, Sir," he said to the Mog commander.

The Mog introduced himself to Marsh by simply stating his name. "Commander Blassen."

In the meantime, Wells was explaining to Gerroll what to do.

"Darrisillite compound, Dr. Wells?" Gerroll questioned.

"Yes, Gerroll. The captain had me inject the girls with it. He had a feeling this was going to happen. This way, we can trace them. He didn't want any homing devices on their clothes or skin in case that…that… whatever he is, searched them. The compound is harmless, but easily traceable if you know what to look for."

"I understand," Gerroll said. He programmed the Darrisillite into his main computer and got an immediate fix on the girls. For now, however, there was nothing he could do. The Mog ship had its shields raised, and the Polaris's transporter couldn't penetrate them to transport the girls out.

"Commander Blassen, just what are you planning to do with the girls?" Marsh asked. He didn't really expect an explanation, but tried anyway. If nothing else, it would buy him some time.

"My options are numerous, Captain," Blassen said, not moving from his position that held the girls restrained.

Marsh gave the theory he and Gerroll had worked out to see Blassen's response. "Give them to the Frazons in repayment for the loss of one of their own?"

Blassen was impressed with the illustrious Captain Marsh. "Good, Captain. Yes, one very high-ranking general, the father of one of the men killed when the Frazon ship was destroyed, wants revenge against your counterpart."

Marsh nodded his head and continued. "But you brought the girls through the portal into this universe instead. Where, of course, they have no counterparts." Blassen's expression told him he was right on target. "Why double cross this high-ranking general?" he asked the Mog commander.

Blassen wondered how Marsh knew all this, but it really didn't matter. "He already paid us," he told Marsh, proud of what he had accomplished.

Marsh was surprised that Blassen was admitting the truth. He must be very sure of himself and his plan. It was amazing what people will tell you when they think they are invincible. Marsh continued on, hoping to get as much information as he could. Knowledge, after all, was power.

"Why would he pay you in advance?" Marsh asked, purposely sounding skeptical.

"We told him that we needed their camouflage technology to combat you, or rather your counterpart, that is."

"I see. And now that you've got the camouflage technology, you can sell the girls again. Very clever, Blassen," Marsh said, and gave his most impressed look.

"Yes, I have a very interested buyer." Blassen smiled leeringly as he looked from one girl to another, still holding them tightly. Then he made a horrible sound, a high-pitched cackle that ripped through Marsh's insides. "He will have a great deal of fun with them!" Blassen added wickedly.

Not with my *girls, he won't,* Marsh thought.

"Blassen, if it's wealth you want, I can give you more LUP space credits than you'll ever know what to do with." It was worth a try.

For a split second, Blassen even considered it. He might be a greedy man, but he wasn't a stupid one. The Mog commander knew that Marsh was trying to buy time, not the girls. He needed to go. Now. Immediately. Get the girls to Jastar, get his space credits, and disappear before Marsh, in either universe, could find him. This transaction would set him for life.

"Thank you for your offer, Captain, but no thank you," Blassen sneered. Then he disappeared from the viewscreen, and the Mog ship disappeared from space as the camouflage device was activated.

Marsh dashed to the science station. "Gerroll, have you got a fix on the girls."

"Yes, Captain."

"Can you transport them out?" he asked impatiently.

"No. The Mog ship still has their shields up."

Damn. Blassen's not taking any chances this time, Marsh realized.

"Can you follow?" Marsh asked, his mind racing.

"Yes."

"At an undetectable range?"

"No. Being in range to detect the Darrisillite compound will also put us in range of their sensors."

Marsh contemplated this. "If we follow them while they are camouflaged, they will know the girls have some sort of homing device. I don't want the girls harmed in any way."

"Of course not, Captain."

"For a while, Blassen will assume that our trail is just luck, so we have a little time to think of something. Gerroll, can you give me details of their ship?"

"Yes. I scanned while you and Commander Blassen were negotiating."

Negotiations that I lost.

"Their ship is a small science vessel. Only twelve crewmembers. Strong phaser power, but only a small complement of torpedoes. Their engines are quite sophisticated, though. A configuration I am not familiar with."

"Gerroll, your opinion. Where are they headed? Blassen said he had a buyer for them." The thought made Marsh sick.

"They have to stay on this side of the portal. In this universe."

"Explain."

"The girls have no counterparts in this universe. Besides, the other universe holds too many risks—the general and the girls' father. This side only has you."

"Only?" Marsh asked with mock hurt.

Gerroll smiled. "A rather large error in judgment, Captain."

Marsh chuckled. "Thank you, Gerroll. Go on."

"Our readings indicate that he is headed into a very isolated sector of LUP space. A perfect location for his…buyer."

"Can you pinpoint a probable planet?"

Gerroll put a map of the sector on his viewscreen and studied it. "Actually, Captain, there is only one planet that fits the criteria for which we are searching. As far as we know, this planet is habitable, although inhospitable—hostile weather conditions all year-round. All of the other planets in that sector would be unable to sustain human life. If Blassen's bringing the girls into that sector, it is logical to assume that he's taking them to a planet where the girls can at least breathe the atmosphere."

Marsh nodded. Could he risk Diane and Robin's lives on this assumption? What if he's wrong and he loses them? It was a hard decision.

"Okay, Gerroll. Let's hope that's the planet."

Marsh walked over to his navigator. "Ensign Todd, reduce speed to hyperspeed 2. Keep us out of sensor range."

Todd was surprised. So surprised that he questioned

the order before he realized what he was saying. "But Captain, once we lose the Mog ship and they remain camouflaged, we may not be able to pick up their trail again." He, like everyone else on the ship, had become very fond of the girls and didn't want to do anything that might jeopardize their safety.

"I'm aware of that, Ensign," Marsh barked. "Do it."

"Yes, Sir," Todd said, relieved that Marsh hadn't reprimanded him for questioning an order.

Wells was also bothered by the captain's decision. "You're taking a very big risk with their lives, Bill."

Marsh understood everyone's concern. "I know, Matt. But I don't have a choice. I don't trust Blassen. I'm afraid he'll harm the girls if he thinks we're trailing him."

"Gerroll, how long to…to…Does that planet have a name?"

"Six hours, eight minutes. It's the planet Jastar, Captain."

CHAPTER 29

JASTAR

It was a very long six hours until they reached Jastar. They had lost Blassen's trail hours before, and now they had to hope they were on the correct course.

"Standard orbit, Lieutenant Walker. Gerroll, scan the surface. Can you find the girls?"

It seemed an eternity to wait while Gerroll searched.

Gerroll spoke slowly as he scanned. "Scanner reading Darrisillite compound coming from…" he paused to recheck his readings "two sources, Captain."

Marsh couldn't help but smile. "Any sign of the Mog ship?"

"Not a trace, Sir."

Marsh shook his head. "No, I wouldn't think Blassen would stick around very long. He probably dropped the girls off, got his payment, and hightailed it out of there.

"Lieutenant Diska, notify the transporter room

that we are transporting down. Gerroll, come with me. Matt, get a medical kit just in case the girls are hurt and meet us in the transporter room."

Kate was waiting when they got to the transporter room.

"Set the coordinates close to the girls' readings, but far enough away so that we won't be spotted," Marsh commanded.

"Yes, Captain."

The three officers stepped onto the platform.

"Ready, Kate?" Marsh asked.

Kate hesitated. "Bill, bring Diane and Robin back safe and sound."

"I intend to do just that," Marsh said and smiled.

She nodded and sent them to the planet's surface.

They materialized in a narrow corridor inside a dark, cold, damp building. The air was thick, musty, and difficult to breathe. They could hear the wind howling outside.

"Looks like an old castle of some sort," Wells observed, looking around. He wrapped his arms around himself in defense of the chill. "Where is everybody?"

"Are you reading any life signs, Gerroll?" Marsh asked.

Gerroll already had his scanner out and was scanning the area. He pointed down the corridor to their left. "Numerous life-form readings in that direction, but no Darrisillite." He continued to scan. "Darrisillite being detected in...that direction," he said and pointed in the opposite direction, to their right.

They walked slowly, watching and listening for any sign of the girls. Wells stopped and craned his neck. "Bill, listen," he whispered.

A very faint sound was coming from up ahead. As they got closer, the sound got louder. By the time they rounded the corner they could hear the yelling.

It was clearly the voices of Diane and Robin, screaming in protest. Marsh was shocked at the foul language he heard. Wow, the last one came from Diane. He'd have to ask her where she learned *that* word.

Despite his concern for the girls' safety, Wells chuckled as he said, "It sounds as if the girls are winning. They're definitely giving him a run for his money. Maybe if we wait awhile, that guy will pay *us* to take them back. Listen to those words! They sure have quite an extensive vocabulary."

"Well," Marsh said, "at least they saved it for an appropriate time." He turned to Gerroll. "How many inside?"

"I'm only reading the girls and one other life form. Not human."

"Let's try to take him by surprise. Is the door locked?" Marsh asked anxiously while listening to the yelling and screaming on the other side.

Gerroll gingerly turned the ornately carved knob. "No, Captain."

Marsh was relieved. What a treat for things to go

smoothly for once. "Well, my friends, I guess we've just been invited in."

All three barged in at the same time, phasers drawn.

The room was large and decadently furnished. Sumptuous red couches and pillows sat on beautifully manicured gold rugs. Thick, gold brocade drapes hung from the windows, and lavish artwork covered the walls.

In the front of the room, sitting on a throne-like chair was a Puserite. Marsh had seen pictures, but had never seen one in person, until now. The alien's face was covered with brown and orange bumps that surrounded pink eyes. The rest of his skin was a sickly shade of yellow. But it was his four arms, two on each side, sticking out of the long brown cape he wore, that gave Marsh the shivers.

The Puserite had a girl on either side of him, holding each securely with one of the arms, while the other arms tried to subdue his captives. Diane and Robin, however, were fighting so hard he couldn't do anything.

Marsh stepped forward and aimed his phaser directly at the creature. "Let them go," he said evenly.

The Puserite stared at Marsh and snickered. "You must be their uncle," he said in a low, gravelly voice as he pulled the girls in front of him to use as a shield. "They told me about you, but they are mine now. Paid for in full."

Gerroll and Wells fanned out on either side of Marsh, but no one could get a clear shot because the creature kept moving the girls to keep himself protected.

"Stop where you are!" the Puserite yelled to the

three officers as he rose to his feet. From behind his stocky body, a long, scaly tail emerged brandishing a weapon, which he aimed at Marsh.

Marsh lowered his phaser, as did Gerroll and Wells.

Diane and Robin screamed—loud piercing screeches that startled the Puserite for a split second.

But that was all the time Marsh needed. Without hesitation, he aimed his phaser, and hit the Puserite in the chest, stunning him. As he fell and his grip loosened, the girls pried all four of his hands off them and ran straight into Marsh's arms. They grabbed onto him and hung on for dear life.

"Matt!" Marsh called urgently to his medical officer, who already had his medical scanner out.

"They seem to be fine, Bill, but I'll check them thoroughly when we are back on the ship."

Marsh tried to hit his communication badge while attempting to maneuver around the girls who wouldn't let go of him. "Marsh to Polaris."

"Lieutenant Diska here, Captain. The girls…"

"They're fine," Marsh responded. "Have two security guards transported down. We have a guest for the brig."

While they waited for the guards, Marsh kept the girls tightly wrapped in his arms until they stopped shaking. As soon as the guards had the Puserite subdued, they transported him back to the Polaris and into a cell. Then Marsh contacted his head engineer. "Kate, five to transport up…three of us, and two young ladies!"

"Yes, Captain, my pleasure!" Kate said with a sigh of relief.

As they jumped off the transporter, Marsh had each girl by the arm. "Okay, young ladies, I want to know just where you learned that language I heard down there." He was trying to act stern, but had actually been quite proud of the fight they'd put up. He'd have to tell them that…later. But right now, he really was curious as to the origins of their lewd vocabulary.

The girls looked like two naughty children who had just gotten caught with their hands in the cookie jar.

"Movies," Robin said timidly.

Marsh was aghast. "What *kind* of movies are you watching?"

"Old-time films from the twentieth and twenty-first centuries," Diane told him.

"Your father lets you watch those?" he asked in amazement.

Robin fidgeted nervously. "Well, no, not exactly."

"Not exactly?" Marsh repeated. *This should be an interesting explanation,* he thought.

"We got the access code to the computer library files for them," Diane told him. "Please don't tell Dad. He doesn't know. Please," she begged.

It was the first time Marsh had heard either of the girls acknowledge, at least aloud, a statement that suggested they would definitely be going home. "If I never hear any of those words again, I'll consider not telling him. Mind you, I said *consider* not telling him."

"Our destination, Captain?" Ensign Todd asked him.

Marsh had been sitting on the bridge for a few minutes, thinking about his next move. He got up and walked over to Gerroll.

"I assume we're going after Blassen, Captain."

"It's our mission, Gerroll. It's the reason Ambassador Kaner went to bat for us—so we could bring Blassen and his crew to justice. But, 'go after' him? No. I have a feeling Blassen will find us. We just have to be patient and wait."

"Captain?" Gerroll questioned, not understanding his captain's reasoning.

"Blassen might be a vile, disgusting excuse for a living being, Gerroll, but he's not stupid. He knew we would go after the girls, and he knew we would get them. He doesn't care—he got paid. Actually, as far as he's concerned, we did him a favor. He got his space credits, and we put the Puserite in the brig, leaving the girls free again. Now, if Blassen were to get the girls back again…"

Gerroll finished the sentence. "…then he could give them to the general as originally planned and complete that bargain as well."

Marsh nodded. "That's right. Then he never has to worry about the general's wrath for double-crossing him."

"He still has to worry about not one, but two Marshes, though."

"Well, Gerroll, life isn't perfect. Who knows, maybe Blassen considers us the lesser of two evils."

"In which case, I hope we never meet this general!"

"That makes two of us," Marsh said and turned toward navigation. "Ensign Todd, set a course back toward Frazon space. Slow…hyperspeed 1. Lieutenant Walker, raise the shields and keep them raised." He wanted Blassen to find them, but no way was he giving up his girls again.

"Hyperspeed 1, Captain?" Gerroll asked, surprised at the slow speed.

"Yes. I want to give Blassen all the time he needs to find us. If we have to fight him, I'd prefer it be on our side of the boundary line."

Marsh contacted Wells in the sickbay.

"The girls are fine, Bill. A few scratches and bruises, but nothing to worry about. Where do you want them?"

"Keep them in the sickbay. I'm expecting some trouble, and it's the safest part of the ship."

"I don't suppose you have any ideas on how to accomplish that?" Wells inquired jokingly.

"I'm sorry, Matt," Marsh said, laughing. "I know that won't be an easy task, but it's where I want them."

"I'll try, Bill," Wells answered, wondering just how he was going to manage this feat.

"One hour, nineteen minutes until we reach the boundary line, Captain."

Marsh had been expecting Blassen to find them by now. Maybe he had overestimated the Mog commander. Perhaps Blassen was just going to disappear without trying to appease the general, after all. In which case, the Polaris would cross into Frazon space in search of the portal that would bring the girls back to their home universe. That would be too bad. Aside from wanting Blassen, Marsh had wanted something else too.

The intercom broke his train of thought. "Uncle Bill?"

"What is it, Robin?"

"We've been here for eons. Can't we come up to the bridge? Just for a little while?"

"It hasn't been quite *that* long, Robin. No, stay put. That's an order."

"It feels like eons, and Dr. Wells is getting grouchy."

Marsh laughed and wondered just what those two had done to make the most even-tempered man he knew grouchy. "Sorry, girls. Play a game with him. That might help."

"Very funny. Don't give up your day job, Uncle Bill," Diane advised him.

"Behave! Marsh out." He had to admit that they did make him laugh…sometimes.

"Captain, Blassen's found us!" Gerroll reported loudly.

The first phaser hit as soon as the Mog ship materialized.

"He's targeting the shields, Captain," Gerroll yelled.

"Keep those shields up, Lieutenant Walker. He wants the girls. If he can penetrate the shields, he will be able to transport them out." Marsh hit the intercom and called the engine room. "Kate, keep diverting power to the shields. We can't let him get his transporter through." He turned to his second-in-command. "Gerroll, I want that ship."

"I know, Captain. Don't worry, their weapons are no match for ours."

"No, Gerroll, I mean…I want that ship! In one piece and operational. We're going to take the girls home in it."

Gerroll understood instantly, and he smiled at Marsh's ingenuity.

"I want his shields off-line," Marsh said, "so we can transport over and capture their ship. But I don't want the ship damaged. Can you do it?"

"I believe so. Give me a minute." Gerroll immediately busied himself calculating the coordinates for the phaser blast that would break through the Mog shields.

"Captain, Lieutenant Wells is reporting that our shields are down to eighty percent," Lieutenant Diska told him.

"Captain, should we return fire?" Lieutenant Walker asked.

"Not until I say so."

The Mog kept firing at them. Each phaser hit sent the Polaris rolling.

"Gerroll…"

"Shields down to seventy percent, but holding," Lieutenant Diska shouted. "Reports of minor damage to decks thirty-seven and forty-six coming in!"

"Bill?" yelled Dr. Wells through the intercom. "What's going on up there?"

"Not now, Matt. Just keep the girls safe!" Marsh yelled back and broke the connection.

"Shields down to sixty percent, and Lieutenant Wells says the engines are straining. If she keeps diverting power to the shields…"

"Keep those shields up!" Marsh commanded as he tried to steady himself from the last blast. "Gerroll…" He was getting impatient.

"Here, Captain," Gerroll pointed to his schematic of the Mog ship. "If we target a phaser blast at precisely these coordinates, I believe we can knock their shields out."

"Will it damage their ship?"

"Minor damage possibly, but fixable."

"Do it!"

Gerroll leaned over Lieutenant Walker's shoulder and programmed the phaser banks to target the area that would take down the Mog ship's shields. "Done, Captain."

"FIRE!"

"Yes!" Ensign Todd roared and threw his arm up in triumph. "Their shields are down, Captain," he announced victoriously.

But the phaser blasts kept coming. Marsh could hear Lieutenant Diska responding as damage reports were called in. "Shields down to fifty percent," she told Marsh. "Lieutenant Wells says there was a direct hit on our engines. We have impulse power only."

A few more blasts and Blassen would knock out the Polaris's shields. Then he would be able to find the girls and take them. Marsh grabbed onto the back of his command chair and waited for the bridge to stop tossing. "Gerroll, we need to work fast," he yelled and Gerroll nodded. "Kate, is the transporter operational?"

"Barely," she reported.

"How many people can transport over to the Mog ship?"

"Three…four if you're into praying."

"Gerroll, I need you here. Have three security guards meet me in the transporter room on the double. I want to transport directly onto the Mog's bridge. How many people are there?"

Gerroll scanned. "Four."

"Good, we're evenly matched, and hopefully we have the element of surprise. Give Kate the coordinates."

Marsh met the guards in the transporter room and gave his instructions. "Set your phasers to stun and fire the moment we materialize. Let's just hope that they are not expecting us. Okay, Kate, send us over."

They materialized on the Mog's bridge a few seconds later. The bridge crew looked up, startled, and drew their weapons. But it was too late. Instantly Marsh's men opened fire and three of the Mog crew toppled, stunned unconscious.

That left Blassen, who had fallen to the floor so he could hide. Marsh dropped and rolled in Blassen's direction and, when he stood up, he was directly in front of the Mog commander. He kicked the weapon out of Blassen's hand and targeted his phaser directly on the Mog's chest, but didn't fire.

"Shoot anyone who comes through that door," Marsh said to his security guards and pointed to the entrance to the Mog's bridge. Then he turned to the Mog commander. "Commander Blassen, it is a pleasure to finally meet you in person."

"The pleasure's all mine, Captain Marsh," Blassen said and smirked.

Stunning Blassen with his phaser would be too easy and not especially satisfying. In one fluid motion, Marsh attached his phaser to his belt and punched Blassen in the gut. The punch was so swift and well placed that even Blassen's huge size couldn't offer him any defense. As he doubled over, Marsh said, "That one's for me." The next punch was a fast left to Blassen's jaw. "That one's for the girls' father, who I'm sure would rather have done it himself." A quick right sent Blassen flat on the floor. "And that one's for the girls."

Now *that* was satisfying. Marsh tapped his communication badge. "Lieutenant Wells, send over a security team. The brig will be hopping tonight! And transport me back. Now."

Marsh sat in the sickbay while Matt attended to his bruised knuckles, which had taken the brunt of his clash with Blassen. The girls were enthralled with his tale, and relieved that Blassen was no longer a threat.

"Are you sure Uncle Bill doesn't need an injector… or two?" Robin asked Dr. Wells.

"No, I'm saving them all for you and Diane," Wells replied, sounding as evil as he could. The girls shuddered and giggled at the same time.

"Now what, Uncle Bill?" Diane asked. She winced when she looked at his hand.

"Well, now we can concentrate on getting you two home."

He never noticed before how bright their smiles were.

"Lieutenant Diska, contact Starbase Sesta VI and advise them the Polaris will be coming in for repairs, and that we have prisoners for them." Ironically, that's where the girls had been not that long ago, trying to convince the communications officer that he was their father. Marsh shook his head to dislodge *that* thought. "Then contact Admiral Packard and keep her up to date.

"Gerroll, you and Kate transport over to the Mog ship and start the repairs. Familiarize yourself with their controls and check the computer logs for the exact coordinates of the portal. Also, see if you can extract the records for all of the kidnapped infants and have them transmitted to Ambassador Kaner on Saras. I want him to be able to locate every one of them and return them to their rightful parents," Marsh said.

"Oh, and make sure you know how the camouflage device works in case we need it."

"Yes, Captain. How many crewmembers will we be taking?" Gerroll asked.

"Just seven," Marsh replied. "That should be enough

to run a small science vessel. I'm sure Kate would rather stay here and see to the repairs on the Polaris, but I want her with us. You never know what problems we might encounter."

Aside from giving them the coordinates to the portal, Marsh was hoping that the Mog ship would help furnish them safe passage through Frazon space. The Polaris would have been like a red flag waved in front of a bull, but the Mog ship would probably go unmolested.

While repairs were made and before they crossed into Frazon space, Marsh had one bittersweet call to make. "Lieutenant Diska, get my parents in New Mexico for me and have the girls meet me in my quarters."

"…and then Uncle Bill captured the Mog ship!" Diane said, finishing the story.

The girls had been talking nonstop for minutes, their excitement making them sound like children at least half their age. Marsh was astonished that his parents were even able to follow what the girls were saying.

"We'll be leaving shortly," Marsh told his parents. "I wanted you to know what was happening and to give you and the girls a chance to say goodbye."

A selfish part of Sarah and Jake Marsh wanted the girls to remain and to be a part of their lives. They were glad, however, that despite the bumps along the way, things had worked out and the girls would be going home.

"We'll miss you both very much," Sarah said, her voice catching in her throat.

"Yes, we will," Jake agreed, putting his arm around his wife. "But we are very happy for you."

"We'll miss you too," Diane said. The excitement had changed to sadness at the thought of having to say goodbye to these people who had done so much for them. Teardrops were sliding down her face. She turned and buried her head in Marsh's chest.

Robin's tears were choking her words. "Thank you for…for…helping us…and…and…for being…" She couldn't finish and she hid her face in his shoulder. Both girls were now crying instead of talking. Marsh looked at his parents, not sure of what to say.

"It's okay, Bill," his mother told him. "They are understandably emotional."

"Yes, I've noticed that." So had his shirt. He'd have to put on a dry one.

"When the girls first came," Sarah Marsh explained, "they were literally a universe apart from us. But they found people who cared for them and who they cared about too. The gap between our universes is shrinking, Bill. We are no longer a universe apart from them. Yes, there are still differences, but now we're only, maybe…a world apart. See them safely back to their world."

Her quiet wisdom always amazed him. "I will, Mom."

"Contact us when you return," his father said.

Sarah watched her son, the mighty Captain William Marsh, hold the two crying girls, and just before the connection was broken, she caught the tender kiss he placed on each head. She couldn't help but think that his rough edges had indeed begun to soften.

As Marsh held the girls, he realized that as much as he had tried to deny it, there was a connection between them, no matter how distant or convoluted it was—a thin thread that crossed the universes and bound them together.

He stood in the quiet room and thought it best to just let them cry.

CHAPTER 30

Unstoppable Together

Matt Wells sat in the captain's quarters and listened to the conversation his friend was having with Ambassador Kaner. Wells had brought Marsh something medicinal to sip and, while he was at it, had brought some for himself too. Hopefully, it would help to ease their anxiety a bit.

"We're headed for Frazon space now, Ambassador Kaner," Marsh was saying. "I just wanted to thank you for your help."

"It was my pleasure, Captain Marsh. I wasn't sure my interference would help, but I knew it wouldn't hurt to try. I'm glad it worked out."

"So am I, Sir. I'm confident that we will find my daughters and the Mog ship. When we do, we will do our best to find the locations of the children that were kidnapped from your outposts."

"Then it will be my turn to thank you, Captain. Good luck." Marsh nodded as Kaner's face disappeared from the viewscreen.

"We could use the luck," Wells murmured. "Crossing into Frazon space makes me nervous."

"Me, too, Matt. But if that's where the girls are, that's where we're going." He took a gulp of the green liquid in his glass. "Good stuff!"

Wells smiled. "Yes, it is," he agreed, and then turned serious. "Bill, do you honestly think that the girls are in another universe?" he asked. "The whole thing sounds so wild to me. A parallel universe? Really?"

Marsh leaned back in his chair. "Gerroll and I have been throwing around a lot of theories and possibilities and, yes, we really do believe, as crazy as it seems, that the girls have been taken into a parallel universe."

"So we're going to cross through that portal Kaner told us about."

"Yes."

"That's if we make it that far. Who knows what will happen with Frazons crawling around all over the place." Wells finished his glass of green liquid and refilled it.

"Gerroll says this sector is relatively quiet. Maybe we'll get lucky." Marsh held out his glass to Wells for a refill too. The two friends sat in silence for a few minutes, both deep in thought.

"We'll find them, Bill," Wells said, reading the tortured look on his friend's face.

"I keep telling myself that. I don't dare allow any other thoughts to get in the way. But my mind keeps drifting to thoughts of 'what if'... and I can't bear the images that pop up. It's just too scary, Matt." Marsh leaned in closer to the doctor and whispered, afraid that if he voiced his thoughts too loudly, it would make them real. "What if they're *not* okay? What if they're *not* coming home?"

Wells refused to consider that possibility. He raised his glass and said, "To the girls, Bill...and their homecoming."

Marsh held his glass up to meet Wells's and then swallowed the smooth liquid in one gulp.

"Besides," Matt continued brightly, trying to bolster his friend's mood, "I wouldn't be the least bit surprised if the girls were talking their way out of the situation. You know how they love to talk and how persuasive they can be!"

"True," Marsh said and chuckled, "maybe they are using their diplomatic abilities to help them through." He grinned as he remembered their last diplomatic endeavor...

Marsh stretched and walked over to stand behind Gerroll's chair and asked him, "How long until we reach Glaxan?"

"Two hours and twenty-six minutes, Sir."

"Gerroll, do you know anything about this planet?"

"No, Captain. I was planning on doing an information check in a few moments."

"Good. Please fill me in on anything I need to know. I want a full report on the people, customs, and anything that would be helpful in securing space docking privileges for the LUP."

Marsh rubbed his eyes; he was tired and was glad he had Gerroll to do this preliminary work.

"Yes, Captain. I'll get on it right away." Gerroll quickly finished the scan he was doing, and then turned his attention to the computer readout on the planet Glaxan. He read for a while, and what he saw brought an immediate smile to his face.

"What are you smiling at?" Marsh asked curiously, never completely trusting Gerroll when he had that impish look.

"Oh, nothing, Sir," Gerroll replied, still grinning. "Seems like a nice planet." Then he quickly added, "I think you should bring the girls with you."

Marsh was surprised. "The girls? Why?"

"Glaxan is an oxygen-nitrogen planet, very similar to Earth. The girls could probably use some sunshine and fresh air," Gerroll explained. He noticed Marsh staring at him, waiting for a better answer than the one he had just given. "Besides," Gerroll continued, "it says here that Glaxan is very, um…child-oriented. It would probably be in your best diplomatic interests if they were with you."

"Actually, it's not a bad idea," Marsh said, thinking it over. He'd been so busy the past few days he'd hardly seen his daughters at all, except when he stopped in to say good night. "I haven't been able to spend much time with them lately and they would probably enjoy it. What else does the readout say?"

"Glaxan is a highly advanced planet, but very private."

"Private? I wonder why?" Marsh mused. "Do you think this will present a problem securing docking rights?"

Gerroll smiled that smile again, and Marsh got ner-

vous. "Well, Captain, you *might find it difficult, but I'm sure it can be worked out to everyone's satisfaction."*

Marsh pondered Gerroll's cryptic answer, but let it go. He was sure it would all become clear in time.

"Captain, you will have to take the shuttlecraft to the surface instead of the transporter. According to these scans, Glaxan's atmosphere has a highly charged magnetic layer that might interfere with the transporter."

"That's no problem. I'll tell the girls to meet me in the shuttlecraft bay at 1400 hours," Marsh said, glad for the opportunity to take the Argo, his private shuttlecraft.

"Captain, I have to go to the engine room for a while. If you'd like, while I'm on my way, I'll stop and tell the girls about going to Glaxan."

"Oh, sure Gerroll, that would be fine. Thank you," Marsh said, and began to read the report a passing yeoman had just handed him.

Gerroll laughed to himself all the way to the girls' quarters. He buzzed and waited for the door to slide open. When it did, he stepped inside, smiled at the two sisters, and said, "Want to have some fun this afternoon?"

He didn't have to be a wizard to know what their answer would be.

As directed, Diane and Robin met their father in the shuttlecraft bay at exactly 1400 hours. Marsh looked at his daughters, impressed. "You two look lovely," he said. "No doubt you'll be the prettiest girls on the entire planet."

"Thank you, Daddy," they said at the same time, as all three mounted the platform that led into the shuttlecraft.

"It won't be a long trip to the surface. Twenty, twenty-five minutes at the most," Marsh informed them. For the next few minutes, the girls sat in silence as their father piloted the Argo off the Polaris and into space. Once he set the automatic controls, he turned to chat with them. "Excited about going?" he asked.

"Oh, yes," Robin said, and looked at Diane who was nodding in agreement.

"Dad, tell us about the negotiations for the docking privileges," Diane requested.

"It should be pretty standard," Marsh said, surprised that his daughters wanted to know about his diplomatic mission.

"What points will you bring out?" Robin asked very seriously.

"Well, if you really want to know, I will present the Small Committee with the benefits of joining the League of Universal Planets. Hopefully, the benefits will convince them to join the LUP, in exchange for space docking privileges."

"Why is it called the 'Small Committee'?" Robin questioned, then smiled at Diane.

"I don't know, Robin," Marsh answered, noticing the smiles exchanged between the two girls. "I assume it is because there aren't many people on the committee." He paused and contemplated their smiling faces. "What are you two grinning about?"

"Nothing, Dad," Diane said. "How, Dad?" she asked, bringing the conversation back to the negotiation process.

"How will you convince them? What exactly will you say? I mean…isn't it hard? We're just curious."

Marsh spent the next twenty minutes outlining his speech for the girls. He was impressed with the intelligent and insightful questions they asked, and he did his best to answer as precisely as possible. He wondered if he had two budding diplomats. He always enjoyed thinking about what his daughters would do when they grew up. Somehow, though, he never imagined them as diplomats. Robin had many interests and was talented in many areas, but her main interest was geology. She had an intense curiosity and a great thirst for knowledge about the subject, and he could see her devoting her life to the study of rocks and minerals. Diane also had many interests and talents, but nothing he could, as yet, see her doing for a lifetime. He looked at his older daughter, and she smiled at him. It would be fun to see where life took his children, and he was glad he'd be around for the journey.

"Prepare for landing," Marsh announced. "It might get a little bumpy because of the magnetic layer."

The shuttlecraft bounced and rocked as they passed through the static, but the landing was smooth and there were no problems.

"Gerroll said we would be met by two members of the Small Committee," Marsh told his daughters. "Let's see if they are here."

The threesome exited the shuttlecraft, ladies first. The city was beautiful—modern and sleek. As promised, there were two committee members present, and both had an adolescent with them. Marsh judged the children to be *about his daughters' age. Gerroll's assessment had been correct. Before Marsh took another step, the two children, one male and one female, solemnly walked forward to greet the three visitors. Marsh smiled and prepared to return the greeting. His daughters, however, took the lead and met the two Glaxan children. The male and female bowed, and his daughters lowered their heads to receive the greeting.*

"*We are pleased to have you on our planet,*" *the female child said.* "*My name is Keeran and my associate is Aundro.*"

Associate? *Marsh thought.* What an unusual thing for a child to say.

"*Thank you for having us,*" *Diane said, and copied the formality of the introduction.* "*My name is Diane Marsh and this is my associate, Robin Marsh.*"

What on Earth is going on here? *Marsh wondered to himself, but everything was happening so fast he didn't have time to interfere.*

"*Welcome, Diane and Robin Marsh,*" *Aundro said.* "*We look forward to our negotiations.*"

Marsh's mouth fell open, but he closed it quickly, knowing that idiotic expressions do not make for the best diplomacy. He waited, confused and silent, to see what would happen next.

Keeran continued the introductions for Diane and Robin, but ignored Marsh. Turning to the Glaxan adults who were standing quietly behind them, she said, "*May I introduce our attendants, Jennis and Rarten. If you are in need of anything, they will get it for you.*" *Keeran then turned her gaze to Marsh.* "*And this is…*"

"William," Robin said, "our pilot." She couldn't look at Diane and still keep a straight face, and she didn't dare look at her father, so she rigidly kept looking at Keeran and Aundro.

"Welcome, William," Keeran and Aundro said together. Marsh nodded, while debating who to deal with first, Gerroll or his daughters.

"Come with us," Aundro said to Diane and Robin. "The committee is eagerly awaiting your arrival. William may stay behind with Jennis and Rarten."

"That will be fine," Diane assured Aundro. Then she held her breath, turned to her father and, in the most commanding voice she could muster said, "William, remain here."

Marsh's intake of breath was audible even from where the girls stood, but neither girl would look at him nor talk to him. Gerroll had explained the Glaxan rules to them quite clearly before they left the Polaris. Both took a deep breath and followed Keeran and Aundro into the nearby building.

Diane and Robin usually trusted Gerroll implicitly, but at this moment, they were both wondering why they had allowed him to talk them into this harebrained scheme. Gerroll had promised them that their father would laugh, but so far, he didn't seem too amused. They couldn't turn back now, so all they could do was hope for the best and pray that at some point, he would find the humor in all of this.

Marsh watched in amazement as his daughters followed the two Glaxan children into the building. He *immediately hit his communication badge…just wait until he got a hold of Gerroll…but couldn't get anything except static. The magnetic layer in the atmosphere must be preventing communication, he realized. He walked over to Jennis and Rarten.*

"Please explain," Marsh said.

"Explain what?" Jennis inquired.

Marsh didn't know where to start. "The children. Who are they?" His questions were met with blank stares. He tried again. "Who's in charge here?"

"Oh," Jennis said. "Now I understand." She looked at Marsh and smiled. "Keeran and Aundro are in charge… of the Small Committee, that is."

Marsh shook his head. "I'm sorry, but I don't understand."

Rarten explained it for him. "You are not from here. You do not understand our ways. On Glaxan, the young ones rule. From birth to ten years of age, the 'olders' teach the young ones the Glaxan way of life. When a young one reaches ten years, he or she begins with an area of lesser responsibility in ruling. As the young one grows, the area of responsibility grows. Maximum responsibility is reached at the age of twenty years. At twenty-one years, he or she relinquishes responsibility and becomes an 'older.' A committee chooses a mate for them, and they will have two young ones of their own, one male and one female. The process repeats."

"What happens to the 'olders' after their young ones reach ten years of age?" Marsh inquired.

"They become attendants," Rarten answered.

"To your own young ones? Are Keeran and Aundro your young ones?"

"Yes," Jennis replied. She pointed to Rarten. "He is my mate, and Keeran and Aundro are our young ones."

Marsh was fascinated. "Do the young ones still receive instruction?"

"No, they are in charge now," Jennis said. "Our orders come from them."

Marsh shuttered at the idea. "But they are so young," he argued and thought of his girls. "You mean to say that their childhood is over when they reach age ten?"

"Yes," Rarten said. "It is the nature of our society." Neither Jennis nor Rarten asked about Earth's culture, and Marsh decided not to volunteer any information. He didn't want to jeopardize the negotiations by possibly saying the wrong thing. Assuming that the negotiations were still under way. He couldn't believe that Diane and Robin were now responsible for securing the space-docking privileges. How was he going to explain this to Space Central?

The girls had been gone for more than three hours when he, Jennis, and Rarten were summoned into the building. By that time, Marsh had circled the building at least a dozen times and had come up with just as many scenarios for Gerroll's demise.

They were brought into an opulently furnished dining room that was elaborately set for seven people. A worker explained, "The young ones have requested your presence at dinner."

Jennis and Rarten bowed when Keeran and Aundro

entered the dining room. "We are deeply honored by your request," Jennis told them.

"Our esteemed visitors made the request," Aundro explained. "It is customary for them to eat with their attendant."

Despite his earlier feelings, Marsh couldn't help but enjoy this charade. His daughters entered the dining room, stately and in control. He was dying to know the outcome of the negotiations, but he understood the rules. Obviously, it was not his place to ask. He would be told.

Robin glanced at him as she passed. She walked slowly with both hands clasped behind her back. As she passed him, both of her thumbs popped up, giving him the answer he wanted. He couldn't help but laugh, an act that drew immediate disapproval from everyone in the room. And the girls' think I'm strict, *he thought, but quickly stopped laughing and behaved.*

Much to his surprise and delight, Marsh enjoyed the dinner immensely. He didn't eat much and hardly said a word, which was good since he didn't think he was allowed *to speak. His joy was in watching his daughters, and his pride in them blossomed with each passing minute. What he had always known was confirmed...individually, each was a dynamic personality, but together, they were unstoppable.* Maybe they should plan a future of joint ventures instead of individual careers, *he thought, and wondered if the girls had ever considered that possibility.*

Toward the end of the meal, Diane asked their hosts, "Do you have vacation facilities for off-world visitors?"

"Yes," Keeran answered. "There is a lovely resort not far

from the main city. It is where Aundro and I go to relax. The accommodations are beautiful. If you would like to visit, please advise us, and we will make sure that you have the best facilities. William may come too. There are small communal huts for the attendants."

"I don't think so!" Marsh heard himself say, and all eyes turned to him.

"He's quite rude," Keeran said to Diane and Robin.

Diane sighed, exasperated. "Yes, he is, isn't he? It's so hard to get good help these days. Sometimes we just don't know what to do with him."

"Will he be reprimanded?" Rarten asked, so seriously, that neither Diane nor Robin knew how to respond.

A devilish smile crossed Robin's face. "Yes, he will have to be," she said, and Diane nodded in agreement. The thoughts that went through the sisters' minds were too good to dismiss quickly, and they sat for a few moments to ponder the sweet scenarios. Visions of confining him to his quarters and taking away his privileges sprang up as quickly as weeds in a field of wildflowers.

"It is a shame when attendants need to be disciplined," Rarten said. "But sometimes it is necessary."

"Yes, sometimes it is necessary. But they must learn," Diane agreed, having a wonderful time at her father's expense. "When we return to our ship," she said sadly, "I'm afraid he'll have to be given…ice cream."

"Ice cream?" Keeran asked. "I am not familiar with that term."

"An old Earth punishment," Robin explained, careful not to look at her father, "very, very unpleasant."

"A shame," Rarten said. "He seems so capable. Perhaps he can be trained."

"There is hope for him," Diane said. "We'll keep him."

Marsh bit the insides of his cheeks. He couldn't remember the last time he was so thoroughly amused.

"Well," Diane said, standing up, "dinner was lovely, but we must be leaving. You will be contacted by another member of the League of Universal Planets to confirm our agreements."

She and Robin bowed to their hosts and Robin said, "It has been a pleasure meeting you. Our worlds will work well together. Thank you for meeting with us."

"It was our pleasure," Rarten said. "Let us walk with you to your shuttlecraft."

The four young ones walked ahead and talked, while the three attendants followed behind in silence.

When Marsh and his daughters entered the shuttlecraft and the door closed securely behind them, they stared at each silently. Then all three burst into uncontrollable, sidesplitting laughter.

"I am so proud of you two," he said as he wiped tears of laughter from his eyes. The three had formed a huddle and were hugging each other tightly. "As for Gerroll," Marsh said, but didn't finish the sentence, not yet sure just what he was going to do with his second-in-command. "Anyway, let's go home."

Gerroll was waiting when the shuttlecraft docked on the Polaris. Marsh looked at the gentle, smiling Nimian and decided what he'd do. Gerroll would have to suffer the same fate that he himself had been given. "Come on,

Gerroll," Marsh said sternly, and put his arm around his second-in-command. "You're going to be punished. An old Earth punishment, and I understand it's very, very, unpleasant!"

"How much longer until we reach the boundary line, Gerroll?" Marsh asked. He was back on the bridge, resting in his chair and feeling a little more relaxed, thanks to Dr. Wells's liquid medicine.

"Twenty-two minutes."

He pushed his intercom button. "Kate, twenty two-minutes."

"We're fine down here, Captain. Ready for anything that comes."

But Marsh was worried. He didn't know why or where the feeling was coming from, but it was there, and he couldn't ignore it. He called each department head and checked in as he had done with Kate. All reported the same as she had...his ship was ready. But was he?

"Crossing into Frazon space now," Gerroll reported.

Marsh watched the viewscreen, his eyes searching for what couldn't be seen—a camouflaged Frazon warship. And he did what he'd gotten so good at doing—he waited.

CHAPTER 31

THE BRIG

"Captain, repairs are completed on the Mog ship," Kate informed Marsh from the engine room on the small vessel. "It's a nice little ship," she added.

Marsh was on the bridge of the Polaris making final arrangements for his journey to bring the girls home. "Good. Did you locate the coordinates of the portal?"

"Yes, we did, and we also found the information on the kidnapped infants. There will be a lot of happy parents. Not only did we find the locations for the four missing Sarasian infants, we also found—Captain, you'd better sit down for this one—information on sixty-seven other infants."

Marsh was glad he was seated. How he'd love to pay a visit to the brig and see Blassen. Only a few minutes! That's all he would need. "And the Polaris?" Marsh questioned, trying to pry his mind off the beast in his brig.

"She needs some more work, but will be fine until

she gets to Starbase Sesta VI. My engineering team knows what to do," Kate reported.

"Thank you, Kate. Great job. As always."

Marsh turned to Gerroll. "Are we ready?"

"Yes, Captain. Lieutenant Diska, Ensign Todd, Lieutenant Walker, and Lieutenant Wells are already aboard the Mog ship. That just leaves, you, myself, Dr. Wells, and, of course, the girls."

"Okay, Gerroll. Have the girls meet us in the transporter room," Marsh said, already on his feet and headed for the hyperlift.

"Where are the girls, Matt?" Marsh asked. He had been pacing the floor of the transporter room for at least five minutes.

"I don't know, Bill. I thought they were with you."

"Gerroll?"

"They were in their quarters. I told them to pack and meet us here."

They waited a few more minutes, and then Marsh leaned over the transporter console and paged the girls' quarters again. Still no response. "Oh, great," he said sarcastically. "After all this, we lose them on our own ship." He pushed the intercom for a ship-wide page. "This is the captain. Diane and Robin, report to the transporter room," he said, and then emphasized the next three words, "ON. THE. DOUBLE!" He drummed his fingers on the console while he waited for the girls to show up. As usual, when those two were involved, he didn't know if he should be worried or angry.

"Gerroll, have the ship's computer locate them."

"Give me a few minutes, Captain. I'll be on the bridge."

Marsh and Wells waited in the transporter room just in case the girls showed up.

Gerroll paged Marsh from the bridge. "Captain."

"Where are they, Gerroll?"

"Sensors show they are in the brig."

Marsh looked at Wells and they both ran. Not wanting the girls anywhere near Blassen, Marsh had forbidden them to go near the brig. *And why hadn't the guard on duty informed him that the girls were there when he heard the page?* Marsh wondered, as they raced through the corridors.

His question was answered when they almost tripped over the body of the fallen guard. Wells bent down to check him. "He's alive, Bill, but not in good shape. I've got to get him to the sickbay."

Marsh waved Wells on and took the phaser off his belt, which he had put there in preparation for transporting over to the Mog ship. Cautiously, he rounded the corner and was met by an all too familiar sight.

Blassen had both girls by the neck. He was standing on the outside of his detention cell, and the force field, which kept the prisoners confined to their cells, was off.

"I can kill them now, Marsh. I have nothing to lose. Drop your weapon."

Marsh let the phaser fall from his hand. "How—"

Blassen explained. "Your girls came to pay me a social visit but got a little too close. I have a high tolerance for your force field, and I grabbed them long enough for them to scream and for the guard to come running. He fired at me but missed, knocking out the force field instead. A very lucky shot, wouldn't you agree? That gave me enough time to snatch your precocious little brats. The nice guard didn't want to jeopardize your lovely girls and foolishly handed me his phaser, which I tested on him. It works nicely, by the way."

Marsh stared into Blassen's gold eyes, searching for any hint of humanity and, not finding any, he turned his attention to the girls. Both were crying. He wished they'd stop.

"I want my ship, Marsh," Blassen said harshly. "Give it back to me and I will give you the girls." He looked from girl to girl. "Are you sure you want them?" he asked scornfully. "They really are an awful lot of trouble."

That was one point Marsh wouldn't argue, but to Blassen he said, "Okay, you win. I want the girls. Give them back to me and I will give you your ship."

Blassen gave an evil, sinister laugh. "You have it backward, Marsh. Ship first, girls later. But I'll tell you what. You can keep everyone else in the brig," he said and indicated the cells full of his crew and the Puserite. "I wouldn't want you to go home empty-handed."

Nothing like loyalty, Marsh thought. "Fine. I'll transport over with you. Just to make sure I get the girls back. Then you're free to go. You know something, Blassen? You're more trouble than *you're* worth." He started for the entranceway.

"No, Captain—site-to-site transport. I'm not walking into a ship full of your crew. Transport me directly to my ship from here. Any games and I will kill them. Trust me, I will, and I will enjoy it too."

Site-to-site transport was, of course, possible, they did it all the time, but Blassen didn't need to know that. "I have to call my second-in-command. He'll have to coordinate it. Our transporter is not as sophisticated as yours," Marsh lied to Blassen, innocently. "We don't usually do site-to-site. People have been known to materialize inside of walls. I'd prefer we didn't."

"So would I," Blassen said sharply. "Go ahead. And also tell him not to send anyone down here or onto my ship." Blassen yanked the girls backwards as he put some distance between himself and Marsh.

"Uncle Bill, help us!" Robin cried, trying to pry Blassen's thick arms off her neck and he yanked her back, hard. She gagged and her arms dropped to her sides.

"Please, let us go!" Diane begged through her tears. She kicked Blassen as hard as she could and suffered the same fate as her sister. She went limp in his arms.

Their cries tore through Marsh, and he had to control himself not to do anything rash that might jeopardize them further. He tapped his communication badge to contact Gerroll.

"Yes, Captain?"

"I need you to arrange a site-to-site transport. Myself, Blassen, and the girls. Transport us directly to…" He looked at Blassen and cocked his head. "Where do you want to go?"

"My bridge."

"…to the Mog's bridge. And please arrange it carefully, Gerroll."

"I understand, Captain."

"Also, don't send any guards down here or transport anyone over to the Mog ship." He looked at Blassen who nodded as he heard the instructions.

"Yes, Sir."

Blassen watched Marsh mistrustfully. He had learned, the hard way, why Marsh had the reputation he had. He wouldn't be one of his victims.

When Blassen turned his head, Marsh looked at the girls and grinned. They knew that grin all too well.

It only took a few seconds for Gerroll to calculate the site-to-site transport and for Marsh, Blassen, and the girls to feel the familiar tingle of the transporter. They materialized, as promised, on the Mog's bridge. Blassen looked around. Empty.

"Smart, Marsh."

"Give me the girls, Blassen, and I'll transport back to the Polaris. Then we'll both go our separate ways." He took a few steps toward the girls.

Blassen tightened his grip on the sisters and they screamed. Marsh stopped moving. "I'd like to. I really would. But that's a bargain I just can't keep," he said as he moved backwards, dragging the girls with him. "You'll only follow and make my life miserable, as if you haven't done so already. No, you all die now. But, I'll finish the girls first so they don't have to watch you die.

Then I'll deliver them to General Malon…dead!" His squeeze on their necks was instantaneous, but luckily, so was Kate's timing.

As per Gerroll's instructions, the three officers that were already aboard the Mog ship—Lieutenant Wells, Lieutenant Walker, and Ensign Todd—were waiting in the corridor behind the bridge entrance. The door slid open and all Marsh could see was the phaser beam that hit Blassen in the back. He ran for the girls as Blassen hit the floor. Diane and Robin were on their knees, desperately gasping for air.

"Marsh to Polaris. Transport Dr. Wells over! Immediately!"

Marsh sat with the girls and waited for the doctor. "Kate, get this guy out of my sight," he said, pointing to Blassen, who had regained consciousness and had three phasers aimed at his head. "Transport him to the Polaris, throw him into the brig, and add two extra security guards to watch him." *And do it quickly*, he thought, *before I decide to take care of him myself, here and now.* Thoughts of what he would like to do filled his mind, each one better than the one before.

Wells materialized in front of him, medical scanner already out and aimed at the girls. He pulled out a pressure injector and used it before any protests could be made, the hissing sound it made completely covered by the girls' sobs.

"Something to help them breathe. They'll be fine," he told Marsh.

"The guard?" Marsh asked, still sitting with the girls.

"Stable for now."

"Good," Marsh said as he got to his feet. He pulled the girls up with him. He held Diane, and Wells held Robin, each man trying to soothe the tears of fright. He spoke above Diane's head, "Is everyone aboard?" he asked the doctor. "It's time to leave."

"Bill, I think the girls should rest in the sickbay for a while."

"They can rest here. I'm sure this ship has a sickbay also. I want the Polaris en route to Starbase Sesta VI as soon as possible, and we have a long journey to make." He looked at both girls and didn't know what to say. His emotions were flying in all different directions, but Robin's question focused him.

"Do you hate us for not listening to you?" she asked. They were breathing a little easier but still crying, although the tears were beginning to subside.

"Hate you? What a silly thing to say. Of course I don't hate you. I'm not happy that you disobeyed me—I won't lie to you, but we will discuss that later." Softly he admitted, "But I'm so glad to see you both safe and sound."

He lifted their tearstained faces so they could see his smile. Hesitantly, they smiled back.

CHAPTER 32

CROSSING OVER

KATE WAS RIGHT, Marsh thought. It was a nice little ship. Blassen had done well fitting it with the most modern luxuries and advanced technologies, which included many they had never seen before and could learn from. Their stay would at least be a comfortable one.

Gerroll, too, was impressed with the small ship and was engrossed in the computer system, gathering as much information as he could from the Mog databases. Lieutenant Walker and Ensign Todd were familiarizing themselves with the navigation stations, laying in the course that would take them to the portal. Lieutenant Diska was monitoring the communication station, studying the new panel and codes that would help them safely through Frazon space. Wells was in the sickbay with the girls, not allowing them to leave until he was sure they had no other injuries from their encounter with Blassen. That was Marsh's first stop after making sure the bridge was running smoothly.

"Well-stocked sickbay, Bill," Matt said as Marsh walked in. "I think I'll borrow some of their instruments."

"Be my guest. That's the least they owe us. How are the girls?"

"They're okay. Shaken up and a little scared of what you're going to do. Want some advice?"

"I know what you're going to say. Don't worry." Marsh looked around. "Where are they?"

"Back there." Wells pointed to a doorway behind him. "There's an infirmary with a few beds. I think I'll keep them there the rest of the day. Just to keep an eye on them."

"Can't imagine why anyone would need to do that," Marsh muttered as he went to find the disobedient sisters.

He found them sitting up in the beds where Wells had put them. They were talking softly to each other, but stopped when Marsh walked in. He looked around and spotted a big, black, cushioned chair lodged against the wall, which he dragged over and placed in between their two beds. The Mog's large size made very comfortable, roomy furniture for humans. He sank into it, trying to look relaxed and put the girls at ease.

"How are you two doing?" he asked quietly.

Both mumbled they were okay. They were very subdued, for once.

"Blassen and his crew are on the way to Starbase Sesta VI for sentencing. They won't bother you or anyone else ever again. You don't have to worry or be afraid anymore."

"We're not, Uncle Bill," Diane assured him.

"Thank you for--" Robin started to say, but he interrupted her with a wave of his hand to dismiss the remark.

"There's nothing to thank me for. Just answer a question for me," he said, looking from girl to girl. "Why did you go see him after I told you not to?"

"We had to. We just had to," Diane said, trying to make him comprehend. "He was the one responsible for bringing us here."

Robin continued. "Now that we're going home, we had to see him one last time. You know, to make sure he was real." She shook her head in frustration, not sure that she was getting her point across. "Does that make any sense? It's hard to explain."

"And to make sure he knew he didn't win," Diane added with a note of satisfaction.

"But we almost blew it," Robin acknowledged contritely.

"Yes, well, it all turned out okay," Marsh said. "I think I understand."

"Now what?" Diane asked him.

"Now, we take you home." *At least we try to*, he thought.

"That's all?" Diane questioned, hopeful, but surprised.

They were both watching him, anticipating the worst for having disobeyed him. Diane was biting the inside of her lip and Robin was playing with one of the curls that had fallen on her face.

"Yes, that's all." He smiled to himself as they looked at each other. "Dr. Wells wants you here the rest of the day." It was an order more than a statement.

"Okay. No problem. We'll stay," they said, talking at the same time. They couldn't get the words out fast enough, and were stumbling all over them in an effort to promise him obedience.

"It might take us a couple of days to reach our destination and I expect—"

"We will," Diane said earnestly.

"Honest," Robin concurred.

Marsh rose, went over to them, and ruffled the curls on both their heads. "Good. I'll see you later."

He passed Wells on the way out, who was still busy checking out the Mog's inventory of equipment. Matt looked up as he saw Marsh. "It was very quiet in there," the doctor said.

"What did you expect, a battle?" Marsh asked him.

"Frankly, yes."

"Oh, ye of little faith!" Marsh said as he strolled out of the sickbay and went back to the bridge to wait for the Frazons.

Marsh liked sitting in Blassen's chair and was sorry Blassen wasn't around to see it. Just to make sure he knew, as Diane had said, that he didn't win. Marsh thought about the victories he'd had over his career. Some had been sweet and some had not. Sometimes victory is necessary, but not pleasant. But this one, he had to admit, was the sweetest of all. Watching Blassen dragged away had been quite agreeable. He thought of the families of the kidnapped children and was glad he and his crew would be a part of reuniting them.

And then Marsh thought of the man waiting in another universe, probably pacing the bridge of his ship, praying for his daughters to come home, doing everything in his power to get them back. "Gerroll!" Marsh called to his second-in-command, as a thought struck him.

Gerroll rushed over to the command chair to give his undivided attention. "Yes, Captain."

"I've been so wrapped up in this universe that I haven't given much thought to what might be happening in the universe we're headed to."

"I'm sorry, Captain, I'm not following you."

"Gerroll, there's another Polaris out there, and another Marsh, trying to find those girls. Your opinion. Where are they? What are they doing?"

Gerroll raised his white eyebrows as he concentrated. He was nodding his head while considering the most plausible theory. Finally, he said, "If we are to assume that the universes are parallel, and the sequence of events is the same in both, at least in most ways, then we would also have to assume that our counterparts have the same information about the Sarasian kidnappings as we have."

Marsh nodded. "So, we can presume that the other Marsh is also headed for the portal."

"Yes, Captain, except that since we were the ones

who captured the Mog ship, we know the coordinates. They do not. Their progress will be slower."

"Hopefully, they will at least be in the general vicinity, and we won't have to go too far out of our way to locate them."

"That would be helpful. Also remember, Captain, that they have no idea where the girls are or what fate has befallen them. They are not looking for us. Everything they are doing is on pure speculation and…hope."

"I know. That's why I'd like to get the girls home as soon as we can. Gerroll, the theories you mentioned about parallel universes. Supposing we do find our counterparts. Can we coexist at the same time, on the same plane with them?"

"The theories differ, Captain. Some say we can exist indefinitely with them, others say not at all."

"That doesn't help me, Gerroll. Your estimation, please."

"In my opinion, we can coexist for a short period of time."

"Define short period."

Gerroll hesitated before answering, no doubt doing some sort of calculations in his head. "To be on the safe side, I'd have to say a few days at the most."

Marsh was relieved. "More than enough time to find them, return the girls, and return home."

"Yes, but I could be in error."

"I'll take my chances. I have no other choice. How long until we reach the portal?"

"Approximately twenty-two hours."

By the next morning, the girls were feeling fine and Dr. Wells had reluctantly let them leave the sickbay. Anticipation about going home was reaching its peak, and they were having a hard time concentrating or sitting still. They wandered the ship, with permission, of course, and found themselves in the detention area where they were originally imprisoned. Neither would step foot inside the cell, and they stood and stared at it from the outside.

"It seems like so long ago," Robin said as they both remembered the three horrible days they had spent there. Those had been the worst days of their lives. It was hard to believe it had only been a couple of weeks ago. So much had happened since then.

At dinner the night before, with danger out of the way, Marsh had told Diane and Robin all about Blassen, his occupation, and why they had been kidnapped. The girls had been right to be scared of him. Never before had they heard of children being kidnapped for anything, let alone a profit. Marsh had promised that with Blassen removed, they'd never hear of it again. At least he hoped they wouldn't.

The Mog ship was in an isolated sector of space and had gone undisturbed so far. Lieutenant Diska had been adept at answering the few hails they received by using the intergalactic translator and the codes she and Gerroll had broken. Marsh was sure the Polaris would not have made it this far. Still, they were all apprehensive, detection only a second away at all times.

Marsh allowed the girls to come up to the bridge and was glad he did. Their chatter took everyone's mind off the travel through Frazon space. Ironically, he remembered how their talking drove him crazy on the shuttlecraft, and now he didn't want them to stop.

"Captain, we will reach the portal in eight minutes," Gerroll reported.

"Thank you, Gerroll."

"Can we stay?" Diane asked hopefully.

"What can we expect, Gerroll?" Marsh asked, concerned for the girls' safety.

"I'm not sure, Captain. Probably just some turbulence."

Marsh agreed to let them stay. He wanted them where he could make sure they were okay.

"Portal coming into view," Ensign Todd announced.

Marsh carefully watched the viewscreen, his eyes searching for anything that might obstruct their entry into the portal.

They all stared at the portal that would take them into another universe. It looked like an everyday, run-of-the-mill nebula—swirling gases that formed a multicolored haze. No wonder no one expected it to be anything other than what it looked like. And, since going through a nebula wreaks havoc with instruments and readouts, it's easier to go around it than through it. Especially considering this one was a small and easy to circumvent.

Marsh held his breath. The girls held hands.

"Entering the portal now, Captain," Gerroll said.

They felt the effects immediately. Aside from the typical rough ride of going through a nebula, they also felt dizzy and disoriented, the influence of crossing from one universe to another. It didn't last long, and the girls remembered the feeling from the first time they crossed over. Except then they had no idea what it meant.

"We're through," Lieutenant Walker yelled and watched his panel. A few seconds later he announced, "Instruments returning to normal."

Diane and Robin stood up and stared at the viewscreen, not searching for danger as Marsh had, but staring at the space that was their home. It didn't look any different, yet the difference was immeasurable. They were completely overwhelmed, and could do nothing but stare.

"How will we find Dad?" Diane asked, her voice a mere whisper.

Marsh didn't answer at first, thinking how he wanted to handle the question. He decided to tell them the truth. Anything could happen from this point on, and the possibility remained that the girls would have to return home with him instead.

"I don't know," he admitted. "We think he will be headed in the same direction, at least we hope so. That's what I would do." He smiled at them, and they smiled back. "Now we head into LUP space and hope that we find him somewhere along the way." He looked at them earnestly. "I'm sorry, but that's the best answer I can give you."

Robin closed her eyes and asked the question she was afraid to even think about. "What...what if we don't find him?" Her eyes stung with tears at the thought.

Marsh held his breath. *Give them the truth*, he reminded himself. "Then you will return to my universe and be a part of my family."

Diane and Robin understood what Marsh was trying to tell them. The possibility still existed that they would never see their father again. They appreciated his honesty, even if it wasn't the answer they wanted to hear.

CHAPTER 33

Dad Heads to the Portal

Marsh watched the stars from his command chair. If he only knew what he was looking for. If he only knew where the Mog ship had taken his daughters. If…if…if. He needed answers to so many questions.

Ambassador Kaner had given Marsh the description of the Mog ship that the Sarasians had gotten from their prisoner, but Marsh doubted the girls were still aboard. It wasn't much to go on, and it seemed like they were feeling their way blindly, not sure where they were going or what they might stumble across in the process.

They had crossed into Frazon space and, so far, had gone unnoticed. Marsh spent his time alternating between sitting and pacing. The bridge crew was quiet and tense, none of the usual chatter that usually accompanied their missions.

"How much longer to the portal, Gerroll?"

"Five hours, ten minutes, Captain."

Matt had been on the bridge most of the time, not only to keep his friend company, but also because he was uneasy about being in Frazon space. At least on the bridge, he'd be informed, whereas in the sickbay he had no idea what was happening.

Lieutenant Walker broke the silence with the words everyone hoped they wouldn't have to hear. "Captain, Frazon warship materializing," he yelled.

Marsh straightened and leaned on the rail behind his command chair, watching the viewscreen in front of him. He spoke quickly and loudly. "Shields up, Lieutenant Walker. Priority 1 alert. Lieutenant Diska, open all hailing frequencies."

"Frequencies open, Sir."

He spoke evenly but authoritatively. "This is Captain William Marsh of the Starship Polaris. Our mission is a peaceful rescue mission…"

"They are firing phasers, Captain," Lieutenant Walker shouted.

"Evasive maneuvers," Marsh shouted as his thoughts jumped ahead to his next step.

The blast barely missed them.

"Guess they're not into diplomacy, Bill," Wells noted.

"Guess not, Matt. Arm phasers, Lieutenant Walker."

"Armed and ready, Sir."

Marsh walked over and stood behind Walker. He waited, waited a bit longer, and then yelled, "FIRE!"

"Direct hit, but their shields are holding," Ensign

Todd reported, and then shouted and pointed to the viewscreen, "Captain, look, the ship is disappearing."

The Frazon ship vanished before Ensign Todd finished the sentence.

"Looks like this is going to be a game of cat and mouse," Marsh said. "But they'll be forced to become visible in order to fire. Lieutenant Walker, hard about. He'll try to attack from the rear."

Sure enough, as soon as they maneuvered around, the Frazon ship was reappearing and firing. The Polaris lunged from the hit and for a second they all lost their balance.

"No damage. Shields holding," Ensign Todd advised him.

"Return fire, Lieutenant Walker. Continue evasive maneuvers."

Blasts fired continuously from the Frazon ship, but the Polaris moved deftly through space in an attempt to avoid them. They took some hard hits but were able to block others.

"Minor damage reports coming in," Lieutenant Diska told him. Marsh assimilated the news but didn't comment, his mind concentrated elsewhere.

"Continue firing, Lieutenant Walker."

"He's disappearing again," Ensign Todd said. The Polaris quieted as the blasts stopped, giving them a short reprieve to regroup.

Marsh went to stand with his second-in-command. "Gerroll, can they continue to camouflage and uncamouflage that quickly? Aren't they expending a lot of energy?"

"Yes, Captain."

"Their weapons are equal to ours. Why would they continue to waste their energy in such an unproductive manner?" Marsh wondered aloud.

Gerroll was staring at the viewscreen. "That's why, Captain. They were just biding time."

Marsh looked up and saw what Gerroll saw. Now there were not one, but two Frazon warships materializing in front of his eyes.

CHAPTER 34

ATTACK

"Captain, sensors picking up three vessels ahead," Gerroll shouted from the small area that was the science station on the Mog ship.

"Frazon?" Marsh asked, and hoped that the answer would be negative.

"Too soon to tell. We are not in range yet."

"How long?"

"One minute, fifteen seconds."

"Matt, take the girls down to the sickbay and keep them there." To the girls he said, "Stay there. I don't want any problems. Do you understand?" He didn't have time to argue and they knew it, so they simply nodded their heads in compliance and followed Dr. Wells to the hyperlift.

"Captain," Gerroll said excitedly. His tone made everyone look up. "Sensors show two Frazon warships and one LUP starship! Readings indicate that it is…the Polaris!"

Marsh tried not to react but found it impossible. *We found them, we actually found them!* He turned quickly to see if Matt and the girls had left the bridge and almost called them back to tell them the news, but then thought better of it. There were still so many variables they had to overcome and he didn't want to get their hopes up.

"Situation?"

"Not good, Captain. The Polaris is under attack from both Frazon warships, although she is still intact and maneuvering."

"Let's hope the Frazons are too busy to have detected us. I want to get in closer. Can you activate the camouflage device, Gerroll?"

"Yes. It will only take a few seconds."

"Do it," Marsh said, then waited anxiously for confirmation.

"Done, Captain. Camouflage device operational."

Marsh nodded. "Bring us in as close as you can so I can evaluate the situation."

As they came into visual range, they could see the Polaris being blasted by torpedoes. She was returning fire at both Frazon warships and maneuvering as best she could under the circumstances.

"What do your sensors show, Gerroll?"

"The Polaris's shields are down to forty percent, but holding. Engines are off-line. She has impulse power only. Life support systems still functioning."

Hold on for a few more minutes, Marsh thought. Then he addressed his bridge crew to inform them of his plan. "When we materialize, the Frazons will believe that we, a Mog ship, happened into this sector by chance, and that we will, of course, help *them*. Upon materializing, commence firing on the Polaris, Lieutenant Walker, but please make sure you miss. Just make it look good. We've got to convince the Frazons we are their allies before we can be of any help to the Polaris."

"My pleasure, Captain," Lieutenant Walker replied, smiling broadly, enjoying the idea of the deception.

Marsh gave Lieutenant Diska her orders. "As soon as Lieutenant Walker begins firing on the Polaris, open a channel to the Frazons—no visual contact, for obvious reasons—and let them know that we are here to help. Use the intergalactic translator and the ship's language banks. Promise our never-ending allegiance if you have to, but convince them we are on their side." Diska nodded while thinking about how to pull that off. "Then," Marsh continued, "hail the Polaris. Use the Beta Code." As an afterthought he added, "And Lieutenant Diska, put that one on visual."

"Ensign Todd, you…you just stay put until I tell you what to do."

"Yes, Sir. I can handle that," Ensign Todd replied and smiled one of his bright smiles that helped break the tension.

Marsh exhaled. "Okay, Gerroll. Uncloak us."

The charade had begun. But this was far from a game.

CHAPTER 35

THE CHARADE

Marsh didn't know how many more hits the Polaris could take. Shields were down to forty percent, the engines were off-line, and he was maneuvering on impulse power only. Kate was doing everything she could to keep them mobile, but even she was going to run out of answers soon. Damage reports were coming in from all decks, and the sickbay was reporting injuries to the crew—luckily only minor so far.

Gerroll looked at his sensors and rechecked them, just to make sure the information was correct before he informed the captain. "Another ship is materializing, Sir."

Marsh shook his head. He'd been hoping for a bit of luck, but things were going downhill fast. "Another Frazon warship to join the party?"

"Negative, Captain."

Marsh's head snapped up. "What then?"

"Based on the information we have, I'd say it was the Mog ship."

Marsh's eyes brightened. *The Mog ship? Could they still have his girls? No, that wouldn't make sense. Why kidnap them, keep them all this time, and then bring them back to him? Something wasn't right here.*

"The Mog ship is firing phasers, Captain," Lieutenant Walker exclaimed, and then smirked. "Lousy shot. He missed! All of his shots are missing!"

Well, Marsh thought, *we'll take the luck any way we can get it.*

"Lieutenant Walker, target the Mog ship and fire on my command."

"Yes, Sir."

Lieutenant Diska called to him from communications, but her voice had an uncertain ring to it. "We're being hailed, Captain."

"Ignore it, Lieutenant, it's just the Frazons looking for surrender."

"No, Captain, it's the Mog ship. Using the Beta Code, and they are requesting visual contact."

To the best of his knowledge, the Frazons had not broken the Beta Code. How could the Mog ship use it? Marsh glanced at his second-in-command. "A trick, Gerroll?"

Gerroll didn't answer. He, too, was baffled, his thoughts echoing his commanding officer's. He also wondered about the girls, but didn't believe that they would still be on that ship.

Matt, on the other hand, was never speechless. "Don't trust them, Bill."

Marsh heard his friend's advice, but disagreed. "It won't hurt to listen, Matt." *Then, when I'm satisfied my girls are not on that ship, and I've learned everything I can, I'll blow them to smithereens.* "Lieutenant Diska, open a channel, and put them on visual. I'd like to see what they look like." *Those monsters who took my children.*

The viewscreen flickered and what they saw held them speechless. Marsh stood, as if to get a closer look. He stared at his own face and saw Gerroll, Lieutenant Walker, Ensign Todd, and Lieutenant Diska looking back at him from the bridge of an alien ship. He had to look around his own bridge to make sure his crew was still with him. There were only two words he could say to the captain looking back at him, for he knew instinctively why that man was there. "My daughters?"

"They're fine," the mirror image responded. "We've brought them home. They are in the sickbay with Dr. Wells, where it is safe."

Marsh could only nod and fight to keep his emotions in check while he listened to the delighted murmurs of his crew. He heard Lieutenant Diska gasp behind him as she stared in shock at seeing herself on the viewscreen, and in elation for the girls' return.

The other Marsh on the Mog ship brought them all back to the problem at hand. "It looks as if you could use some help."

"All that we can get," Marsh admitted, but knew everything would be okay despite the pounding his ship was taking. He hadn't come this far, his daughters now within his reach, to be defeated by the Frazons. He was suddenly able to think with a clarity he hadn't felt in weeks.

"We have convinced the Frazons that we are here to help them," said the other Marsh from the Mog's bridge. "That should help keep them off guard for a while,"

"Yeah," Ensign Todd said, "While they try to figure out why you're such a lousy shot." His counterpart laughed.

"Captain," said the Polaris commander to his counterpart on the Mog's ship, "I think we'd better do this without visual contact. It seems to be a bit too distracting."

"Agreed."

The Polaris's commander signaled to Lieutenant Diska to shut off visual contact, which brought the stars and the Frazons back into view, leaving them with voice contact only. He was startled by the sound of his counterpart's voice—the same as his own—when he heard him say, "If we target the main engines at the same time, my Gerroll says we can take them out." Marsh looked at his Gerroll, who nodded his agreement.

"I will coordinate the target point with their second-in-command," Gerroll said from his station on the Polaris.

While the two Gerrolls conferred, Matt came over and whispered in the captain's ear, "Told you, Bill." He raised an imaginary glass to remind his friend of their discussion, and repeated his original words..."Here's to the girls' homecoming."

"To their homecoming," Marsh echoed, and smiled up at his friend. He was having a hard time believing that the wait was finally over.

Gerroll finished his communication with his counterpart on the Mog ship, walked over to Lieutenant Walker's station, and set the proper coordinates. "Ready, Captain," he announced when he had finished.

"Okay, Gerroll. It's all yours. Do it!"

"Fire on my command, Lieutenant Walker," Gerroll told him. "We're ready when you are," he said to his counterpart on the Mog ship.

"We're ready! FIRE!" his lookalike on the Mog ship replied.

"Now, Lieutenant Walker! FIRE!" Gerroll repeated.

They all watched as the blasts came from both the Polaris and the tiny Mog ship. The torpedoes found their target, and the first Frazon ship exploded in a blaze that lit their screen. The second Frazon ship was close enough to catch some of the fire, and the two Gerrolls once again coordinated their efforts to finish it off.

But not before the second Frazon ship, now realizing the Mog's ship was not on their side, was able to fire off one last torpedo—straight at the tiny ship. The crew on the Mog's bridge saw the blast coming and watched the bright ball of light and energy as it got closer and closer.

"SHIELDS UP! BRACE FOR IMPACT!" Marsh shouted from his command chair on the Mog ship, and they took hold of anything they could. The torpedo struck with a force that sent them all tumbling to the floor.

Marsh stood up slowly and surveyed the bridge of the Mog ship. Smoke was coming from some of the panels, but no one seemed to be hurt.

He hit his intercom. "Matt!" he yelled, praying they were all okay. No response. This time he screamed his friend's name. "MATT!"

"Here, Bill. We're okay. The girls are fine. What's happening?"

Marsh sighed. "It's all good, Matt. Trust me, it's all good. Marsh out." He turned his attention to Gerroll. "Damage?"

"Enough. But we still have to take out the second Frazon ship before they fire again. It has been damaged and is responding slowly, but it is still operational. The other Gerroll and I are coordinating it now." He went back to his communication with his counterpart on the Polaris. It only took a few seconds. "We are ready, Captain."

"Go ahead, Gerroll! Do it! Take that ship out!"

Again they watched as the Polaris and the Mog ship fired simultaneously. The second Frazon ship exploded, leaving only a trail of debris. Both crews, on both ships, took a few minutes to sit back and relax.

It was finally time to reunite Diane and Robin with their father.

CHAPTER 36

HOMECOMING

Marsh, Gerroll, Dr. Wells, and the girls materialized in the Polaris's transporter room. Marsh would have sworn it was his ship, but standing at the console was his counterpart, and his bearing made it perfectly clear this was *his* Polaris.

The girls jumped down and rushed into their father's waiting arms with such force they almost knocked him over. The trio left on the transporter platform joyfully watched the reunion and found it hard not to be drawn into the heartwarming scene. The quiet room allowed them to hear the joyous words of homecoming and love, along with the sobs of emotions finally released.

As the father held his daughters, Marsh watched as unabashed tears rolled down his counterpart's cheeks. It shocked him to see this on the face so like his own. He tried to remember the last time he had cried, had shed a tear for anything, and it bothered him that he couldn't.

Still holding his daughters tightly, the father greeted his visitors. He looked at his counterpart and, knowing there would never be words to express his gratitude, simply said, "Thank you for bringing my daughters home."

"It was my pleasure…" Marsh began, and then stopped. He wanted to call this man something, but didn't know what. It was like looking in a mirror. How does one address oneself? He let the sentence trail off, unresolved.

"We're not safe in Frazon space," the captain of this Polaris reminded his guests. "We'll keep the Mog ship in our tractor beam and head back to LUP space where we can finish all repairs. Both ships need work, but between our two chief engineer's coordinated efforts, it shouldn't take too long, a day at the most. Why don't you stay here until the repairs are finished? We can… um…get acquainted," he said and laughed, also at a loss for words.

"I think we'd all like that. I know I would," Marsh admitted. He'd been in some strange situations, but this one topped the list.

The father looked down at his daughters. It was so good to see them, to hold them, to know they were okay. He kissed them both again and wondered if he'd ever be able to get enough of them. "The sickbay is your first stop," he told them. "Dr. Wells is waiting for you."

"We're fine, Daddy," Robin argued, still snuggled in her father's arms. "This Dr. Wells has already checked us out."

"Really, Daddy, we're okay," Diane agreed. She, too, hadn't moved from the safety of his embrace.

The girls were reluctant to leave their father's side and he knew it. He was reluctant to let them go.

"Well, *our* Dr. Wells won't be satisfied until he's done it himself." He smiled and winked at the doctor next to him, figuring he would understand, and turned back to his girls. "Besides, I think our Dr. Wells would like to say hello. And then later, I want to hear every single detail about the last couple of weeks. Okay?"

Diane and Robin still hesitated.

"Come on you two," Wells said, trying to pry them away from their father. "Let's see who's better looking, your Dr. Wells or me."

The girls shook their heads and smiled at the doctor's silliness. "We'll go with him, Dad," Diane said. "Just to make sure he stays out of trouble."

"Good idea," their father agreed, and chuckled, then looked at Gerroll and declared, "There's someone on the bridge looking forward to meeting you too."

Gerroll's impish grin made them all laugh. "I think I can find my way," he said, still snickering as he headed for the door.

"See you later, Gerroll," his captain called to him. "Have a good time!"

Gerroll turned around to face the two captains, his white braid swinging gently against his back, his eyes sparkling, "Trust me, Captain, I will!" Then he left to find his counterpart.

"We can transport Diska, Walker, and Todd over

whenever you want." The captain of this Polaris knew that his Kate Wells would never leave a damaged ship, and therefore assumed that her counterpart wouldn't, either.

"Right now, they're helping Kate, but acting like children who have to do their chores before they can come out and play," Marsh said, thinking of the disappointed faces he got when he told them they had to stay and see to the repairs on the Mog ship.

"I'll send my Kate and a crew over to help them. This way they can finish faster and still have time to play!" this captain said with amusement, then asked his counterpart, "Can I offer you a drink?"

"Oh, I think I could use one," Marsh admitted.

"Yeah, me too. My quarters?"

"Sure, I think I know the way."

Marsh walked the corridors as if they were his own. The route was the same and everything was familiar, including the faces of the crewmembers who passed him.

The crew had been apprised of the situation, but they couldn't help but stare at the duplicate captains as they passed, and it was evident from the looks on their faces that they couldn't tell which man was their own commander. Neither Marsh gave any indication of who was who, and when they reached their destination, they both started laughing like schoolboys. Feeling like naughty identical twins who were trading places for the day, the two captains had to admit they were having a grand time.

They settled into comfortable chairs, stared at each other, and began to talk at the same moment. Time flew as they relived shared memories and heard about adventures experienced by each individually. They talked about family and friends, amazed at the likeness of their worlds and fascinated by the differences.

Marsh heard all about Daniel, the brother he never had, and found himself wishing he had known him. He thought of his mother and how sad she had been at the mention of the name. But it was also because of Daniel and the girls' reference to him that his parents had finally believed their story and contacted him. That thought reminded him of his mother's request. "My mother requested I give you a message. She said to tell you that you did a great job raising the girls." Marsh paused, then added, "My parents became very close to Diane and Robin, and vice versa." He went on to tell his counterpart how his parents wanted to raise the girls if he wasn't able to get them home.

The father was overwhelmed. "Please, there are no words to thank them for what they did, but do try anyway—for me and for *my* parents."

"I will. Too bad our parents can't meet. According to the girls, they are exactly the same. It would be quite an experience."

The father shook his head in agreement. As soon as they were within communication range, he'd have Diane and Robin contact their grandparents. He couldn't wait to see the thrilled expression on their faces!

Knowing his daughters the way he did, the girls'

father dreaded asking the next question. "Did the girls give you any trouble?"

"No, not exactly," Marsh said, "but I must admit that it took me a while to get used to the role of 'Uncle Bill.'"

The father had wondered what his daughters had called this man who looked just like him. His ego was glad that they hadn't called him 'Daddy,' although he would certainly have understood if they had.

"There *was* the pizza pie incident," Marsh said, trying to think of the most innocent example of the girls' mischief.

"Oh, no, they didn't," the father said, shaking his head in disbelief, but chuckling, nonetheless.

"They did," Marsh confirmed. "And I was promptly reminded by headquarters that the unofficial use of a distress call is against Space Central regulations!"

"Yes, I got the same warning when they pulled that one here!" the father said. "What did *you* do?" he inquired, curious how this man who wasn't used to being a father, handled the situation.

"I ordered pizza for dinner and then sent them to their quarters for the remainder of the night."

The father was surprised and not surprised at the same time. "That's just what I did!"

"I know, they told me afterwards," Marsh said, remembering their valiant arguments to change his mind.

"Is that all they did?" the father asked. He would be relieved if that was the extent of their mischief, but he knew his daughters better than that.

Marsh opened his mouth to answer, then closed it, deciding not to say anything yet. It would all come out as the story they told unfolded. Instead, he shrugged noncommittally.

"I see," the father said knowingly. "It must have been an interesting couple of weeks for you."

Marsh nodded and grinned. "You could say that again!"

The father talked about his daughters and shared the tales of their youth, their practical jokes and their pranks, all stories beginning enthusiastically with, "And then there was the time…"

Despite himself, Marsh laughed and realized that he had seen only the tip of the iceberg. He also knew that he would miss the girls. It would take him a while to get used to the quiet on the ship.

The intercom buzzed, taking them each from their thoughts.

"Marsh here," said the commander of this Polaris.

"Captain, I just wanted you to know that the repairs are coming along fine," Kate reported. "They should be finished sometime tomorrow."

"Thank you, Kate. Marsh out." He looked at the time and was shocked. "We've talked through the whole afternoon. I'm starved. Let's go have some dinner. I want to hear the girls' tale." He stopped and thought for a second, and then asked, "I wonder where they are?"

Marsh was relieved to hear he wasn't the only one who went around asking that question.

Dinner was great fun and extremely unusual, to say the least. Seven sets of counterparts and the girls. When people started to filter in, the room began to take on the air of a Halloween party, the rule being you had to come dressed as a twin.

Marsh might have been captain of this ship, but honestly couldn't tell his crewmembers from those of the Mog ship. He confessed that to his counterpart, the only person in the room, apart from his daughters, of whose identity he was certain.

"Don't ask me," his counterpart said. "I wanted to talk to Matt, but I don't know which is which, and I'm too embarrassed to ask!"

Diane and Robin were standing against the wall watching.

"Hey, Rob, look quickly. Which one is Dad?"

"The one on the…left. No, the right…left. I don't know," she finally admitted. They both burst out laughing as they tried to figure it out.

"Imagine living with both of them," Diane suggested.

"Imagine getting in trouble with both of them," Robin countered.

They pondered the implications of *that* scenario.

During dinner, the girls sat on either side of their father and recounted their tale in every minute detail. Well, almost every detail. It was amazing how they managed to forget the times they didn't behave. It only took a clearing of Uncle Bill's throat to jog their memories, and eventually it all came out. In reward for their truthfulness, he kept his word and didn't say anything about the computer access code they had broken for the movies they really shouldn't be watching. He knew their father would find out eventually.

Toward the end of dinner, they got a call from the bridge informing them that they had crossed the boundary line and were now back in LUP space. A cheer went up around the table, and everyone sighed and gave their own silent prayer of thanks.

"May we go to the rec room?" Diane asked her father when dinner was over. "We heard that all of our friends will be there for a welcome home party."

"Then I guess it would be rude of me to keep away the guests of honor, wouldn't it?" their father asked playfully and nodded his permission.

The girls said their good nights and dashed out, eager to spend time with the friends they had missed so much the last couple of weeks.

Eventually, the group split up, each of the counterparts headed in a separate direction, looking forward to talking and learning more about one another. The two captains ended up in the main lounge. They made their way through the crowd of off-duty personnel to the front of the room, and sat in front of the viewing window.

The father laughed and shook his head. "If only I had known," he said in retrospect. He didn't look at his counterpart sitting directly across from him, but stared out at the stars instead. "I spent two weeks going out of my mind with worry, imagining things no parent should ever have to imagine. While all along they were safe with you…driving you crazy."

"I have to admit, they did at first, but then, as I got to know them and…" Marsh let the sentence linger, half finished. That was the beauty of having a counterpart—he understood the unfinished thought.

The men chatted and philosophized, and gradually the lounge began to empty. By midnight, they were alone, still talking, and unaware of the quiet around them. The sound of Diane and Robin coming in interrupted them.

The girls looked at the two men seated and, if not for the assumption that their father would take his usual chair, they otherwise would not have known who was who. The assumption was confirmed when he spoke.

"It's late," their father said softly, "And it's been a long day for you."

"We'll go soon. Can we stay with you for just a little while?" Diane asked him.

It was a request he would not refuse, tonight, or any other night. He nodded, as they knew he would. The girls walked toward him but, as if by design, they changed their minds at the same moment. They would have a lifetime of sitting with him and they would take advantage of every second of it. But tonight was different. Instead, they went to the chair across from him. Quietly, they sat down and snuggled on each side of the man they had called 'uncle' for the last two weeks.

The father smiled. As always, he was so proud of his daughters.

The uncle smiled too, and he securely wrapped an arm around each girl and pulled her close. Within minutes, Diane and Robin were asleep—safe and secure in the arms of the man who had brought them home.

Marsh savored each second. Tomorrow, he would begin the journey back to his own, lonely universe.

The End

ABOUT THE AUTHOR

The Captain's Daughters is Doreen D. Berger's first novel in a series about the adventures of the Marsh sisters, Diane and Robin. Doreen, known to her family and friends as Diane, has based the series on her relationship with her lifelong friend, Robin, and their spirited childhood escapades. Doreen lives on Long Island with her family and pets.

Doreen welcomes your comments and questions! Please visit DianeandRobin.com

Soon to be released…Diane and Robin's next adventure…*Reach for the Stars*